MW01221989

PENNSYLVANIA
AN ILLUSTRATED HISTORY

PENNSYLVANIA
AN ILLUSTRATED HISTORY

Donald E. Markle

LIBRARY OF
CONGRESS
SURPLUS
DUPLICATE
NOT FOR RESALE

HIPPOCRENE BOOKS, INC.
New York

Copyright © 2009 Donald E. Markle

All rights reserved.

For information, address:
  Hippocrene Books, Inc.
  171 Madison Ave.
  New York, NY 10016
  www.hippocrenebooks.com

Library of Congress Cataloging-in-Publication Data

  Markle, Donald E.
    Pennsylvania : an illustrated history / Donald E. Markle.
      p. cm.
    Includes bibliographical references and index.
    ISBN 978-0-7818-1197-2 (alk. paper)
      1. Pennsylvania—History. 2. Pennsylvania—History—Pictorial works.
    I. Title.

  F149.M366 2009
  974.8—dc22   2009001023

Printed in the United States of America.

DUPLICATE
NOT FOR RESALE

4-12-2014
amazon.com mktplc.
(Bookmonger Ltd)
$3.49 + $3.99 SH

Dedicated to
all the proud citizens
of
the state of Pennsylvania

Pennsylvania state coat of arms.

The Pennsylvania state coat of arms was designed in 1778 by Philadelphian Caleb Lowness. It was adopted by the state legislature soon thereafter.

The coat of arms consists of the following elements:

- A shield crested with an American eagle, containing a ship, a plough, and three sheaves of wheat
- Two black horses as supporters
- An olive branch and a cornstalk, crossed below the shield
- Under the shield is the state motto: "Virtue, Liberty, and Independence"

Contents

ACKNOWLEDGMENTS

Compiling the history of any state in the United States, especially one as old as Pennsylvania, is no small undertaking. Every native has a story about the state that he or she believes should be included. In addition, each of the sixty-seven counties has its own personal history, and while all are of interest, they do not necessarily contribute to an overall history of the state. I have tried to balance the wide range of inputs to create a history of the state of Pennsylvania, which may create more questions than answers, and I believe that is a good thing. If this history sparks an interest to learn more about a particular facet of Pennsylvania's history, I have been successful. The history has a full range of interest areas—for all readers.

In compiling this history, I am indebted to the multitude of historical societies we have in Pennsylvania—both state and local. Every society I contacted was willing to supply me with the knowledge base of their historical archives. I would also like to thank State Representative Steve Maitland and his staff, who gave me access to his extensive holdings of books on the history of our state. It was most helpful.

My special thanks to the Governor's Office and the Pennsylvania State Department, who allowed me to use the reproductions of the state coat of arms and the official seal in the book. Martha Brown and Catherine Ennis of the Pennsylvania State Department were particularly helpful in providing the necessary graphics.

And last but by no means least; I would like to thank two people who were both supportive and critical as I progressed through the history. First is my wife, Geri, who happens to be a fantastic proofreader, and second is Mr. Arthur Thimsen, who has a great grasp of history and a sense of how it should be told.

INTRODUCTION

The history of Pennsylvania evolved initially out of its central location in the colonial period and is driven largely by the state's natural resources.

The state, although one of the original thirteen colonies, was not one of the early settlements in the New World. Its charter was not granted until 1681—seventy-four years after the first settlement at Jamestown. That does not mean that there were no Europeans living in the area now known as Pennsylvania—Swedish emigrants had settled there as early as 1638.

During the early colonial period, Pennsylvania, like the other colonies, had largely internal interests; the state was supreme, and each state developed its own character. In the case of Pennsylvania, that character was initially closely associated with the city of Philadelphia. This city represented the cultural center of the new colonies with a wealthy class of merchants, a thriving seaport, and such assets as daily newspapers, libraries, and a plethora of intellectual societies. Late in this period, the city grew to be one of the largest cities in the world. For the early American colonists, the geographically central location of Philadelphia made it an ideal choice for when the various colonies wanted to meet as a group. Pennsylvania was synonymous with Philadelphia.

As settlers began to push westward, the state began to undergo considerable change. Vast mineral deposits in the state were being discovered, and industries such as iron production and coal mining developed to exploit the new discoveries. In addition, another city began to be noticed in the western part of the state—Pittsburgh. A rivalry soon arose between the eastern and western parts of Pennsylvania, one that in some forms persists to the present day. Philadelphia remained the cultural capital of the state, while Pittsburgh rapidly became known as the industrial center.

The advent of the War of 1812, the American Civil War, and the Spanish-American War awakened Pennsylvanians to the reality that they not only had a responsibility for their own citizens but that they were also a significant part of the national scene. And with that realization, Pennsylvania entered the modern phase of the state's history.

This particular history concentrates on the internal aspects of Pennsylvania's history while not excluding the state's importance in national events. They are intertwined and cannot be separated.

The history is broken down into periods, initially based on historical events and then later into fifty-year increments. It should be stressed that each county and region has a unique history of its own. This work concentrates on the state as an entity in itself and not its individual parts.

CHAPTER ONE

THE GEOGRAPHY OF PENNSYLVANIA

The geography of the state of Pennsylvania was not always lush valleys, rolling hills, mountains, rivers, and streams. The current landscape has evolved over time, predominately due to the early ice ages and the presence of glaciers. It is estimated that around 16,000 BCE, glaciers covered the northern part of the state with heavy layers of ice. In addition, the Ice Age caused the water level of the Atlantic Ocean to drop, creating an Atlantic coastline approximately two hundred miles east of the present-day coastline. Pennsylvania was originally landlocked. The ice remained until approximately 10,000 BCE, when the glaciers receded, creating new valleys and plains in their paths. This was followed by an extremely cold period from approximately 9,000 to 8,000 BCE, which made it very difficult for plants and animals to survive. Around 8,000 BCE, a global warming trend began, and the final glacier runoffs created the present-day landscape of the state. Another major climatic change occurred between 6,500 and 3,000 BCE, when seasonal climate changes began to appear.

The state of Pennsylvania covers an area of 44,820 square miles, ranking it geographically as the thirty-third largest state, and is sur-rounded by New York, New Jersey, Delaware, Maryland, West Virginia, and Ohio. The average width of the state is 285 miles east to west and 156 miles from north to south. There are 1,239 square miles of water surface within its boundaries. The only natural boundaries of the state are forty miles of the Lake Erie coastline and the Delaware River; all the other boundaries are as proscribed by the charter granted to William Penn by King Charles II (all land between the 39th and 42nd degree north latitude and from the Delaware River west for 5 degrees of longitude). The elevation of the state varies from sea level at Philadelphia to its highest point, Mount Davis, in Somerset County, with an elevation of 3,214 feet.

Originally, Pennsylvania was a transition zone between the northern and the southern primeval forests. On the northern plateau, white pine and hemlock mixed with beech and sugar maple trees flourished, while on the southern plateau, white oak, chestnut, hickory, and chestnut oak trees were prevalent.

Three major river systems flow through the state. All of the major rivers were of sufficient depth to allow for early ship-borne traffic:

- The Delaware River, with tributaries of the Schuylkill and Lehigh rivers, running in a southeasterly direction
- The Susquehanna River, with the tributary of the Juniata River running in a north/south direction
- The Ohio River that begins at the confluence of the Allegheny and the Monongahela rivers, running in a southwest direction.

The land mass of Pennsylvania consists of a series of plateaus (traveling from east to west):

- Piedmont (Lancaster and York counties predominately)
  - Triassic lowlands
- Ridge and Valley Province, composed of:
  - Cumberland Valley
  - Lehigh Valley
  - Wyoming Valley
- Appalachian Plateau
- Lake Erie Coastal Plain

There are two major mountain ranges in Pennsylvania: the Blue or Kilatinny Mountains, which reach a height of one thousand feet, and the Alleghenies, where heights of over three thousand feet are attained. Both ranges are subsequently divided into smaller ranges.

Pennsylvania's soil consists predominantly of three major types: inceptisols, ultisols, and alfisols. Of the three types, alfisol soil is the most suited for agriculture; the other two types require extensive fertilization, making agriculture more difficult. Because alfisol-type soil is found only in the southeastern and southwestern sections of the state, these sections were the breadbasket for early settlers, and they remain predominately agricultural today.

Mineral deposits are found throughout Pennsylvania, which ranks tenth in the nation in production of mineral products. These products are predominately coal, petroleum, natural gas, and cement, with lesser production of fire clay, iron ore, lime, slate, and stone.

One of the smallest of the fifty states, the 2000 census ranked Pennsylvania thirty-third in size and gave the state an official population of 12,291,054 persons. Pennsylvania ranks second highest in the United States in the number of elderly people—sixty-five and older (next to Florida). Of the total state population in 2000, 95.9 percent of residents were born in the United States and 77.7 percent were born within the state of Pennsylvania.

The position of the colony of Pennsylvania, situated between the northern and southern colonies, as well as the shape of the state, gave rise to calling Pennsylvania the "Keystone State." That nickname has survived to the present day, even though the literal translation of Pennsylvania is "Penn's Woods," named for British admiral Sir William Penn, the father of the founder of Pennsylvania, the Quaker William Penn.

CHAPTER TWO

THE NATIVE AMERICAN AGE
(15,000 BCE–1600 CE)

GENERAL HISTORY

Relatively speaking, the arrival of the American Indian in the area now known as Pennsylvania occurred much later than in the western states. The migration from Asia to the Americas began approximately 30,000 years BCE. On the North American continent, migration continued on a southern course, which, unlike the eastern course, was ice free. For Pennsylvania, it is estimated that the Indian migration into the area began around 15,000 years BCE, as the glaciers in the eastern section of present-day America began to recede.

The earliest known archaeological evidence of human habitation in Pennsylvania is the Meadowcroft Rock Shelter south of Pittsburgh. It is estimated that this shelter dates from between 14,000 to 12,000 years BCE (the early Paleo-Indian period). Most of the artifacts found at the site were implements for the processing of fibers, skins, and wood. It is believed that these early settlers were generally not hunters but lived more like migratory scavengers on the natural foods of their environment, such as corn, squash, grains, and berries. However, this changed over time, and by the later Paleo-Indian period (10,000 to 8000 BCE) the local Indians had become game hunters as well.

The movement of the Indians in Pennsylvania was dictated by the state's three main river basins. The Susquehanna and the Delaware rivers ran north and south, giving some Indians a north/south orientation to their expansion. The other river, the Allegheny, ran to the west, and the Indians migrating from the west followed this river and settled along its banks. As the glaciers melted, Indians expanded into the now-inhabitable areas, but they continued to move regularly to be able to harvest natural foods and game. Life was harsh, as the land was semi-barren and only just recovering from glacier ice, and the climate was cold and severe.

Later in the Archaic Era (8000 to 3000 BCE), life became a little easier for the early Pennsylvanians. During this period, seasonal climate changes appeared and, with them, new forests of trees such as oak, which provided acorns for human and animal ingestion. At this time, the Pennsylvania Indians lived and traveled in small bands of about thirty-five to fifty members. The women gathered foodstuffs from the wild, and the men hunted for game. Techniques for hunting advanced as well, and it is from this period that arrowheads and spear points can be found today. The tribes continued to move, and by the end of the Archaic period, all three of the river basins were populated by nomadic Indians. In the case of the Delaware and the Susquehanna, northern migration from the south (predominately from present-day Maryland) continued to increase the population. For the Allegheny Basin Indians, the migration was predominately to and from what today is the Ohio River Basin.

As the warming climate change occurred, around 1000 CE, the Pennsylvania Indians' existence changed accordingly. They became not only hunters but farmers as well. Beans that had been grown in the southern areas of the North American continent now arrived with new Indians as they migrated into the area, soon to be followed by maize and squash. These three staples became known as the "three sisters," and they had a direct impact on Indian life. The trend to agriculture meant that tribes remained in one location, raising crops, and this led to the growth of the concept of a village. A tribe would create a village and remain until the land would no longer produce needed crops—approximately twenty-five years—and then would move to a new location. These were hunter/agriculture societies, but there is no evidence of domesticated animals during this period. As time progressed, the Pennsylvania Indians developed active trading arrangements with other tribes.

Over time, as Indians became more and more dependent on their farm produce, possession of good farmland became an important aspect of their lives. Having not yet developed advanced farming techniques, when the land "wore out," they simply moved to a new area with good, arable land. This led to tribes developing the concept of territorial rights—a concept that also led to increased warfare between rival tribes over land.

Such was the environment in the early 1500s, when the first European explorers arrived. In early Pennsylvania, the white man was not initially looked upon as an enemy but as a new trading partner, with new and unusual trading commodities. The Indians did not realize that along with their initial contact with the white settlers came new threats—the white man's own desire for land and the even more devastating threat of exposure to new European diseases.

Indian Tribes in Pennsylvania at Time of First European Arrival

Indian traditions have it that the original Indian inhabitants of Pennsylvania were the Alligewi Indians who gave their name to the Allegheny Mountains and the Allegheny River. These Indians were driven out by the Lenni Lenape and the Mengwe tribes in the early 1500s CE.

By the time of the arrival of European settlers, the Indian tribes in Pennsylvania were the Eries, the Iroquois Confederacy, Lenapes, Monongahelas, Shawnees, and Susquehannocks.

Eries: Settled in the northwest corner of the state near what became known as Lake Erie. By 1680, they had been subjugated by the Iroquois, and by 1681 the Eries had ceased to exist as an independent tribe.

Iroquois Confederacy: Known initially as the Five Nation Confederacy, Iroquoian-speaking tribes included the Mohawks, Oneidas, Onondagas, Cayugas, and the Senecas (predominately in New York State and upper Pennsylvania).

Lenapes: Lived in the area of the Delaware River Basin (also known as Shenk's Ferry). They developed a unique language and became known as the Unami. Little is known of the Lenapes. They lived in small villages, hunted and fished, and later took to farming. Subsequently, in 1740, they began to migrate to eastern Ohio.

Monongahelas: Lived predominately in an area southwest of Pittsburgh.

Shawnees: Came to Pennsylvania around 1698 from Ohio and settled in the Lancaster area and along the Susquehanna River as far north as the Wyoming Valley. They remained in the state until the middle of the 1700s, when they once again returned to Ohio, when the Iroquois power waned there.

Susquehannocks: An Algonquian-speaking tribe living along the Susquehanna River in Pennsylvania and Maryland. They were a warring tribe, finally destroyed as a nation through continual warfare by 1763. The Susquehannocks settled in the Lancaster County area and were known locally as the Conestogas.

Village Life

The village was normally the domain of the females. Women not only took care of the family but frequently were also part of the tribal leadership. They tended to the agricultural tasks as well as the weaving and other domestic activities, while men hunted. Homes were usually round in shape, made of tree bark or skins, and were arranged in a circular formation to create a village. A notable exception was the Iroquois. Rather than round houses, each clan inhabited a longhouse, often as large as forty feet long and twenty feet wide. An Indian village could be as small as thirty to fifty people or, in the case of the Iroquois, as large as two thousand people with up to 150 buildings.

Tools and Pottery

Digs of Indian settlements from around the end of the Archaic period reveal the presence of rudimentary tools, such as axes and awls, made of stone and largely created by males. As time progressed, so did the tools, later including instruments made of copper.

It is generally believed that Indian women were the potters, and pottery appeared during the late Woodland period (beginning 1000 BCE). The initial pottery was flat-bottomed with straight sides, with a capacity ranging from quart size to several gallons, and was probably used to store grain. Each area had its own distinct versions of pottery,

Shenks Ferry Compound Decorated

Lancaster Incised

Some examples of pottery decorations from the later Woodland period.

both in texture and decoration. The decorating generally consisted of a pattern that would be scratched into the surface of the pot prior to firing.

Over time the pots became rounded on the bottom with curved walls, but the etching of a pattern on the exterior walls continued. As the Indian society became more and more agrarian, the size of the pots increased both for cooking and for storing foodstuffs as well.

Petroglyphs

Creating petroglyphs, or carvings on stone, was common practice among many of the Indian tribes. Some of these petroglyphs have

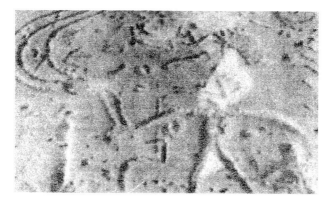

Indian petroglyph from Shenk's Ferry.

been found along the Susquehanna River in the Lancaster area. The carvings were done to convey specific information, possibly a tribe's boundaries or hunting grounds or to signify a sacred place or direction. Their exact meanings are unknown, as is the identification of the specific tribe who created each individual petroglyph. However, current thinking places the time of the petroglyphs during the late Woodland period (1000 BCE) when the Shenk's Ferry culture thrived along the Susquehanna River.

Beliefs

The word *religion* does not exist in any Indian language; however, by traditions handed down through the generations we do know that they did have a belief system that tended to transcend any specific tribe. Tribes believed in a creator of the world as well as various spirits that directed their lives on earth. There is no evidence of a belief in an afterlife.

A basic belief was that the landscape was composed of elements with spiritual powers. For example, the "three sisters of beans, squash and maize" were friendly as they provided substance for the tribes. Animals could be good or bad. The climatic elements were also seen as friendly or evil, depending on how they were treated by Indians. Indians believed that offerings had to be made to placate the spirits. These spirits were generally seen as neutral with the potential for good or evil. If Indians made alliances with these spirits it was felt that the spirits would be friendly to them.

One of the central figures of their spirituality was the tree. They believed it depicted all phases of life—the roots represented the underground, the trunk the real world, and the branches the sky world. It was the divine order in a natural world with roots that went to all four corners of the world. The importance of the tree was clearly evident when the Iroquois Confederacy was formed. A white pine tree was planted as the tree of peace. The five needles became the symbol of the five original tribes joining the Confederacy, and the roots were to spread peace throughout the four corners of the natural world.

Burial practices varied among the tribes. In some cases, burial mounds were utilized. Others practiced individual burial (normally outside of the village). For some tribes, no traces of burial sites have been found.

Astronomy

Native American Indian relics and traditions handed down clearly indicate that the early inhabitants of the Americas had a rudimentary knowledge of astronomy. For example, some tribes buried the dead with their heads to the east, so that they could face the rising sun. There are also early reports of using specific stars for tracking purposes. The exact extent of Pennsylvanian Indians' knowledge of our solar system remains an enigma. At the Slackwater site near Lancaster, there is some evidence of a possible "Woodhenge," or celestial measuring structure. The remnants of this Woodhenge are a series of large post holes surrounding a hearth. The post holes are aligned with the four cardinal directions, based on celestial north. The evidence is inconclusive, but some believe that this Woodhenge is similar to like structures found in the Mississippi Basin.

With the arrival of the white man into their environment in the early 1600s, the Indians' way of life in Pennsylvania changed forever. Although not a great deal of specific knowledge is known of the early Native American inhabitants of Pennsylvania, we do know of their lasting impact on the early settlers. It was the Native Americans who showed the settlers where to hunt for game; introduced the farmers to Native American crops such as beans, squash, and corn; and imparted the knowledge of the geographic features of the land, including the trails to the interior and the locations of water sources. Their assistance was vital to the survival of the early European settlers.

CHAPTER THREE

EUROPEANS ARRIVE IN PENNSYLVANIA

(1609–1681)

The early European explorers of the New World probably did not reach present-day Pennsylvania until the early 1600s. Obviously, the area was not as easily accessible as the Atlantic coast for the various sea-based captains and explorers.

One of the earliest explorers in the area was Captain John Smith of Virginia, who in 1608 journeyed up the Susquehanna River and kept a diary of his meetings with the Susquehannock Indians. No land claims or settlements resulted from his exploration. Such claims came in 1609, when Captain Henry Hudson, an Englishman in Dutch service, sailed into Delaware Bay and claimed the land for the Dutch—later a source of conflict between the Dutch and the Swedes. Hudson's visit was followed in 1610 by that of Captain Samuel Argall of Virginia, who visited the area and named the Delaware Bay in honor of the current governor of Virginia, Lord de La Warr. For the next thirty years, Pennsylvania remained virtually untouched by the presence of the white man—and when the first settlement came, it was not a Quaker settlement but a Swedish one!

In 1626, Sweden decided to establish a settlement in the New World as an investment opportunity by forming the Swedish West India Company. Finally, in 1637, two ships under the command of Peter Minuit arrived in the New World and sailed up the Delaware Bay and the South River. In April of 1638, they successfully negotiated for land with five Lenape chiefs—Nattahorn, Mitatmint, Etu Panke, Mohomen, and Chiton—and the Swedish experiment was born. These early pioneers, while waiting for the permanent settlers, had much to do, and to assist them they recruited slaves, the first of whom arrived in New Sweden in the year of 1639 and was given the name of Anthoni Swartz.

The first permanent Swedish settlers arrived in the New World in 1643, and they established several villages, which included Upland and Fort Christiana (near present-day Wilmington), calling the area New Sweden. They maintained friendly relations with the local Indians, trading with them and negotiating land deals for farming. Within a year, Governor Johan Printz arrived and moved into his home on Tinicum Island (near the site of the present-day Philadelphia airport). New Sweden represented the first permanent European settlement in Pennsylvania, but it did not last. It was founded on the premise that beaver pelts, much in demand in Europe, could be obtained from the Indians and sold in Europe. This premise was faulty. The beaver pelts acquired in the area of Pennsylvania were not as lush as those of more northern climates and therefore not in high demand. The colony faltered, and finally in 1655 Governor Peter Stuyvesant sent Dutch troops into the area and annexed New Sweden to the Dutch territory with no resistance from the Swedish settlers. The Swedish settlement period was over. But little changed until William Penn arrived in 1682.

While short-lived, the Swedish settlement period left a lasting impact in several ways. To name a few of the Swedish accomplishments in the New World, we find the introduction of log cabin construction, the innovation of the keel boat for shallow water, the introduction by a man named Peer Gunnarsson Rambo of the Rambo apple, and the introduction of peaches to the New World. By the early 1700s, peaches had become so common that new settlers believed them to be indigenous to the area.

Sweden sent Lutheran missionaries into the colony, and they continued to thrive there even after the arrival of William Penn. The Swedish branch of Lutheranism is quite close to the Church of England and therefore was not alien to the English settlers when they arrived. The government of Sweden continued to support their missionaries until 1831.

Along with the beneficial impact of the Swedes, there were adverse impacts as well. The settlers brought with them domestic

A Swedish log cabin built along Darby Creek in the seventeenth century.

animals—horses, cattle, pigs, and sheep as well as vermin such as rats, mice, houseflies, and lice. They also brought grain seeds that contained not only wheat and barley but also dandelion, plantain, daisy, and other weeds that were previously unknown in America. The settlers themselves carried diseases previously unknown in the New World, including smallpox, measles, influenza, amoebic dysentery, whooping cough, and malaria. The first epidemic of one of the new diseases in Pennsylvania was recorded in 1642.

The Dutch domination of the area now known as Pennsylvania was also short-lived, lasting only from 1655 to 1664. That year, England's King Charles II granted James, his brother and Duke of York, a patent for all the land that now included New York and New Jersey. To ensure his patent, the Duke of York sent an armed force to the New World, and the Dutch surrendered without a shot. Their domination was over. After 1674, a steady stream of English settlers began settling around the Pennsylvania area.

Swedish influence continued into the early part of the next phase of European settlement. When William Penn arrived to establish his new colony, he first arrived at the Swedish village of Upland, which he promptly renamed Chester. When he wanted land to build his great metropolis, Philadelphia, he bought it from two Swedish brothers named Svensson. Penn initially relied on Swedish settlers as interpreters and agents in dealing with the Indians.

With Penn's arrival and the subsequent arrival of the Quakers, New Sweden began to decline. While tolerated by the Quakers, who believed in freedom of religion, the Swedes were soon a minority and all too quickly forgotten.

Chapter Four

The Quaker Years
(1681–1774)

General History

William Penn, the founder of the state of Pennsylvania, was born in England in 1644. He was the son of a prominent English admiral also named William Penn. Admiral Penn is credited with having prepared, or overseen, the codification of the "Fighting Instructions" of the Royal Navy in 1663. The Fighting Instructions included the code of flag signals used by the Royal Navy up to the adoption of the more sophisticated and flexible numeric codes of the late eighteenth century.

William, the son, matriculated at Oxford but was expelled at the age of seventeen due to his radical ideas. At twenty-two, after meeting John Foxx, he converted to Quakerism, causing considerable concern to his family. For, while Penn enjoyed all the privileges of high status, he constantly railed against the current class structure and what he perceived as dictatorial religious ideas of British society. At the same time, the simple life of his fellow Quakers was not completely accepted by the highborn William Penn. This proved to be a constant dilemma for the remainder of his life, as he liked the Quaker emphasis on the individual but at the same time believed in the strong form of government of Britain.

The beliefs of the Religious Society of Friends, known as Quakers, had a direct impact on the settlers in Pennsylvania. The core of the Society's beliefs is that all are called to minister to one another—there is no church hierarchy. They believed that each individual must find his own spirituality, and it need not be Christ centered. They were free thinkers who followed their own derived ideas.

Penn, both a religious zealot for Quakerism as well as a man who desired to make a fortune for himself, began to search for a location where his fellow Quakers could live their lives in peace. At the same time, he wanted the experiment to be financially rewarding to him. Finally, after ten months of negotiations with England's King Charles II, Penn was granted 45,000 acres of land along the Delaware River, between Lord Baltimore's province in Maryland and the Duke of York's province in New York, in payment of a sixteen-thousand pound debt owed to his father by the king. The land was named Pennsylvania in honor of Admiral William Penn, not his son. The grant was to be the personal property of the Penn family and included land defined as being between the 39th and the 42nd degrees north latitude and from the Delaware River westward for 5 degrees of longitude. In 1682, Penn acquired from the Duke of York his claim to the three lower counties on the Delaware River (now the state of Delaware).

Penn persuaded about six hundred investors to invest in his venture, and in the two years between 1682 and 1684, over fifty ships carrying four thousand immigrants sailed for the new colony of Pennsylvania. Penn arrived in his new colony in 1682 and immediately

William Penn

created three counties (Philadelphia, Chester, and Bucks) and summoned the general assembly to meet in Chester. Here they adopted the *First Frame of Government.* While the colony proved to be economically sound, Penn's financial handling of the revenues was disastrous. Nearly bankrupt, he returned to England in 1684, financial difficulties looming over him for his entire life.

In 1692, due to the Glorious Revolution in England that led to the ouster of James II and the establishment of the reign of William III, Penn had his colony taken away from him. He had been a supporter of James II during the Glorious Revolution and suspected of treason by the followers of William III. The colony was not returned until 1694, when the Crown was restored to the English throne. Penn, who had returned to England in 1684 in an attempt to solidify his financial holdings, returned to his colony in 1699, remaining for a period of two years before once again returning to England.

Later, after returning to England, William Penn testified before the Board of Trade that his venture had cost him about fifty thousand pounds more than he had received. Unable to pay his debts, in 1709 he was sent to a debtor's prison in London, where he remained for nine months. Then released, he discovered that his province had been mortgaged to pay his debts and acquire his freedom. He died a very bitter and dejected man in 1718 after a series of strokes. Upon his death, Mrs. Penn managed the affairs of the province. She was successful in paying all of her husband's debts and was well respected. The Penn family remained in England until 1773, and from then until the American Revolution, a Penn heir, his son John, was the governor of the state. While his colony prospered, William Penn did not.

The initial premise of the Pennsylvania colony was that it would be a haven for religious freedom. Quakers were initially the predominate religion, but by the middle of the eighteenth century the majority shifted to the Lutheran and Presbyterian faiths. This shift to a Protestant majority affected the overall governmental philosophy that all should be willing to take an oath of allegiance to their God; the Quakers were not—their god was personal.

All land acquired was to be bought from Indians through negotiation and treaties. Major land purchases were made by treaties in

1684, 1732, 1737, 1749, and 1768. One of the most important treaties was the Treaty of Lancaster in 1744, when the Six Nations ceded all of their land to the "Setting Sun," meaning to the western edge of the Allegheny Mountains. The colonists continued to push westward, and in 1760 Pennsylvania established the first British settlement west of the Appalachian Mountains at Fort Pitt. By 1768, all of what is now Pennsylvania except for the northwestern portion had been "purchased."

The colony continued to grow, and along with growth came a political phenomenon that remains in the state today. The early settlers in the western, more frontier part of the state were predominately agriculturists, and they soon developed a political rivalry with the eastern part of the state, predominantly populated by tradesmen and other professionals.

Penn's colony enjoyed a relatively peaceful existence with the Indians, but as more and more Indian land disappeared, Indians became more aggressive in nature. Conrad Weiser stands out as the prime negotiator in maintaining peace with the Indians during this period. In his youth, Weiser voluntarily spent the better part of a year with the Iroquois Indians in New York State. He became fluent in their language and understood their way of life.

Statue of Iroquois Chief Shikellany

Soon after the arrival of Penn's provisional secretary James Logan in 1729, Logan became aware of Weiser's knowledge of the Indians and quickly appointed Weiser his chief negotiator with the Indians of Pennsylvania. Conrad Weiser was very successful in his endeavors and continued his efforts until his death in 1760. One of his main Indian supporters was the Iroquois Chief Shikellany, and a statue of Chief Shikellany stands today on the grounds of the Conrad Weiser Homestead at

Womelsdorf, Pennsylvania. When Weiser died, Chief Shikellany said, "We are at a great loss and sit in darkness as since his death we cannot so well understand each other."

The loss of land, coupled with the French aggression in the western part of the state, led to what is now known as the French and Indian War, from 1754 to 1763. This was followed by a later Indian conflict known as Pontiac's War, which began in 1763 and ended in 1766 when Colonel Henry Bouquet defeated the Indians at Bushy Run (southeast of Pittsburgh). In addition, with the large European demand for beaver pelts, wars broke out between various Indian tribes over trapping territory. These wars came to be known as the Beaver Wars. The Beaver Wars, although won by the Iroquois, decimated the Indian tribes.

The land west of the Appalachian Mountains was a continual friction point between the British government and the colonies. The majority of the land east of the mountains had been settled, and settlers wanted to push west. The British government was concerned with the high cost of ensuring the safety of the western settlers, so on October 7, 1763, King George III issued a Royal Proclamation regarding the territory land issue. The proclamation stated that all lands west of the Appalachians were reserved for the various Indian tribes. Settlers were forbidden from settling on these lands, and land negotiations with Indian tribes were forbidden. But the proclamation was not strictly recognized by the colonists, who continued to push west.

GOVERNMENT

When the first English colonists arrived in Pennsylvania, they brought with them a traditional English form of government—that of townships, boroughs, and counties. This form of government was well established in England: the first reference to it dates back to 890 CE.

Upon his arrival in the New World, William Penn, in addition to establishing the state assembly, soon created the first counties in the state for local government. They were Philadelphia, Bucks, and Chester counties. As the population of the state increased, so did the number of counties, eventually arriving at the modern total of sixty-seven. All of these counties have boroughs and townships for local government, just as they did when the state was first settled. By 1773, there were eleven counties. Of them, Westmoreland County was the first county located entirely west of the Allegheny Mountains and the last one chartered before the American Revolution.

The first borough on record in Pennsylvania is Germantown (near Philadelphia). Its borough charter was granted by William Penn in 1689, and it went into effect in 1691. In contrast to the borough government for a city or town, the colonists also established the "township," which was for the more rural areas of the state. So began the long tradition of local government in the state of Pennsylvania. The first major township legislation was enacted on May 18, 1765, when the provisional government under John Penn required the election of supervisors for all townships and an assessment of taxes to maintain township roads. (*Note:* Today Pennsylvania has 1,729 townships and 963 boroughs.)

William Penn was the proprietor of the new colony, even though he spent little time there. He appointed lieutenant governors to serve in his stead as head of the colony's government. Between 1695 and 1777, thirteen individuals served in this role. After William Penn's death, his heirs served as the proprietors of the colony.

The more formal colony government was based on a series of documents known as the *Frame of Government*, written by William Penn. The first of the documents was written in England prior to his arrival in the New World, and was signed on April 25, 1682. This document laid out the structure for the governing of the colony. The preface of *Frame* is also considered to be one of the classic writings on the structure of government. The document established a provincial council of seventy-three popularly elected members to assist the colonial governor, as well as a provincial assembly that met annually to enact the necessary legislation. Further, it structured the judicial system and the criminal code. Until 1756, the provincial assembly was made up predominately of Quakers, but as the immigrant population grew it changed to contain a more representative mix of members.

In addition, the *Frame* granted the right to vote as follows:

- *A purchaser of 100 acres of land, or upwards and every person who had paid his passage and held 100 acres, cultivating at least 10 of them.*
- *Servants or bondsman, free by his service, that shall have taken up his fifty acres of land and cultivated twenty thereof.*
- *Every resident of the colony who pays scot and lot to the government.* ("Scot and lot" was a municipal tax levied on members of a community proportionate to their ability to pay.)

Objections to the *Frame* led to its amendment in April 1683. The *Second Frame* changed the provincial council to three members from each county with a total membership no less than eighteen or more than seventy-three. Also, the governor was given veto power.

This *Second Frame of Government* was amended on November 1, 1696, and became known as the *Markham Frame*, after Governor Markham. One of the main corrections concerned the criteria for voting rights. The new frame stated:

> *That no inhabitant of this province or territories, shall have right of electing, or being elected as aforesaid, unless they be free denizens of this government, and are of the age of twenty-one years or upward, and have fifty acres of land, ten acres whereof being seated and cleared, or be otherwise worth fifty pounds, lawful money of this government, clear estate, and have been resident within this government of the space of two years next before such election.*

The original criteria had actually deprived many of the people living in Philadelphia the right to vote, as most owned no land to speak of. The new amendment corrected this major fault.

Finally in October of 1701, when William Penn was once again residing in his colony, a new, fourth frame was issued. It was known as the *Charter of Privileges* and is noteworthy as it is the first frame for which public input was allowed. The frame began with what has become a famous statement of religious freedom. It states:

> *I doe hereby Grant and Declare that noe person or persons Inhabiting in this Province or Territories who shall Confesse and Acknowledge one Almighty God the Creator upholder and Ruler of the World . . . shall be in any case molested or prejudiced in his or theire person or Estate because of his or theire Conscientious perswasion or practice nor be compelled to frequent or maintaine any Religious Worship place or Ministry contrary to his or theire mind or doe or Suffer any other act or thing contrary to theire Religious perswasion.*

The *Charter of Privilege* also made the assembly a unicameral assembly (a single body of representatives, as opposed to the more typical bicameral, or two-chamber, system). The assembly would have four members from each county, representing the entire population and not just the wealthy, as had previously been the case with the upper chamber. The governor could no longer dissolve the assembly if it did not reflect his views. The charter also made no mention of the council, which thereby ceased to exist as a legislative body and then served strictly as an advisory body for the governor. This fourth frame was to remain in effect until the First State Constitution was adopted in 1776.

With William Penn's subsequent departure for England, political parties began to appear. The main parties that arose were the following:

- The Proprietary Party: Composed of loyal followers of William Penn and led by James Logan, they were predominately the educated and wealthy Quakers in the Philadelphia area.
- The Popular Party: Opposed to the policies of the Proprietary group and in favor of a more democratic society, this group was led by David Lloyd, a Welsh Quaker and lawyer. His influence was second only to that of William Penn.

- **The Non-Quaker Church Party**: Composed of non-Quakers who wanted to make Pennsylvania a royal colony with an established church and a strong military, it was led by Robert Quarry, a judge of the admiralty. Its influence was not significant.

In 1687, not long after the original *Frame of Government* was produced, William Penn produced another governmental idea—this one much bigger than the state of Pennsylvania. In 1697, he wrote the *Plan for a Union of the Colonies in America*. In this document Penn proposed that each colony appoint two deputies who would gather as a group and meet annually at a central location "to hear and adjust all matters of complaint or difference between Province and Province," and to provide for mutual defense. His suggestion was ignored by the colonies.

However, the idea arose again in 1754 when Benjamin Franklin, a Philadelphia scholar and inventor, presented his *Plan for Union* at the Albany Congress. His plan called for the unification of the colonies under a grand council appointed by the colonial assemblies and a president-general who would be appointed by the king. Franklin's plan, like Penn's, was ignored.

Initially, the provincial assembly met wherever convenient, including inns, local Quaker meetinghouses, or private residences, but almost always in the city of Philadelphia. In February of 1729, a petition was presented to the assembly, and by May 1, 1730, a bill appropriating two thousand pounds for the construction of a state capitol building was passed. Finally, in October of 1736, the Assembly of the State of Pennsylvania met in their new capitol building. However, five more years elapsed before the interior of the building was finished. This first Pennsylvania capitol building was to become one of the most famous buildings in America, later taking the name Independence Hall and becoming the home of the Declaration of Independence. It was also the site of the 1775 convention that created the first Pennsylvania state constitution.

The bell—later to become the Liberty Bell—was not installed until 1753. The bell had been ordered by Speaker of the Assembly Isaac Norris to commemorate the fiftieth anniversary of William

Penn's grant. It was also dictated that the bell be cast with the words "Proclaim Liberty thro' all the Land to all the Inhabitants thereof" (from Leviticus 10:25, Christian Bible). The prominent tower was not completed until 1758.

On the first ringing of the bell in 1753, a crack appeared in the brim, fouling its sound. It was recast that same year in Philadelphia by John Pass and John Stow, but the resulting sound was so bad that Pass and Stow recast it again in 1753. The results were still not satisfactory, and finally in November of 1753 an order was sent to Whitechapel in England for a new bell. When it arrived, it did not have a clear sound—it was no better than the one created by Pass and Stow already hanging in the steeple of the State House. The Whitechapel bell did not replace the Pass and Stow bell but was placed in the cupola of the State House. It is generally accepted that the famous "crack" in the Liberty Bell occurred when the bell was rung on February 23, 1846, to commemorate George Washington's one hundredth birthday. The bell did not receive the name of "Liberty Bell" until it went on a national tour in the 1880s.

The Liberty Bell

Independence Hall in Philadelphia

In 1757, Benjamin Franklin was sent to England with instructions to convince the royal government to allow the Pennsylvania colony to tax the proprietary estates. After two years of negotiations, Franklin succeeded in his mission, but he remained in England for another five years. Upon his return to Philadelphia, he was greeted as a hero and almost immediately sent back to England on a new mission. This time it was his charge to have the proprietorship abolished in favor of a Crown Colony, thereby making the colony a British possession and governed by a governor appointed by Parliament. This petition was never actually presented; and as events were moving against its acceptance, the independence movement superseded these demands and made them irrelevant.

In the early 1760s, the relationship between the colonies and England took a drastic turn for the worse. England antagonized the colonies by passing a series of repressive acts, including the Sugar Act, the Currency Act, the Quartering Act, and the now notorious Stamp Act of 1765. These acts had great impact on all of the colonies, and in reaction, nine of the colonies, including Pennsylvania, met in New York for a newly formed "Stamp Act Congress" in October 1765. The Congress approved a Declaration of Rights and Grievances that stated that the colonists were equal to British citizens, objected to taxation without representation, and claimed that the British parliament could not tax the colonies without colonial representation in Parliament.

During this period, Benjamin Franklin began his diplomatic career for the colonies when, in 1757, he was sent to England to represent not only Pennsylvania but also Georgia, New Jersey, and Massachusetts. In 1765, he presented the colonists' grievances to a session of Parliament and succeeded in having the infamous Stamp Act rescinded in 1766. He remained in England until 1775, when he returned to the colonies.

Tension continued, however, with Parliament's passing of the Declaratory Act, which stated they had the power to pass legislation binding the colonies, and the Townshend Act, which instituted levies on glass, lead, paint, paper, and tea. The colonies, including Pennsylvania, decided to follow a policy of non-importation.

Also in 1767, a man named John Dickinson, a Pennsylvania legislator, wrote and published the pamphlet *Letters from a Farmer in*

Pennsylvania to the Inhabitants of the British Colony. The pamphlet may not have had much impact in Britain, but the sentiments expressed by Dickinson, that the colonies were sovereign in governing the various colonies while Parliament had jurisdiction only in matters for the entire British Empire, definitely affected the inhabitants of the colonies. Earlier in 1765, Lawyer Dickinson had become the leader of a political group known as the Half and Half Party—later taking the name Whigs. This group limited its protests to objecting to the Stamp Act and opposed it by sending appeals to the British parliament.

The merchants of Philadelphia, although economically affected by the Townshend Act of 1767, refused for two years to join with fellow merchants in New York and Boston in the Non-Importation Agreement adopted in 1767. The merchants of Philadelphia did finally capitulate and join the embargo, but only after strong pressure was put on them by trades people, artisans, and laborers of Philadelphia.

During the late 1760s and early 1770s, intense competition arose between what became known as the Proprietary and the Quaker elites, predominately in the area of Philadelphia. The Proprietary class was composed of the wealthy merchants whose businesses were suffering due to the strict British tax system, and they wanted change. The Quakers, on the other hand, believed in pacifism and wanted to maintain the status quo, as they saw their political power beginning to weaken. Up until 1756, the Quakers had controlled the Pennsylvania political system, but in that year seven Quaker deputies resigned from the assembly in protest of action taken against the Indians, thereby effectively ending Quaker control of the Pennsylvania Assembly. The political influence of the Quakers was beginning to come to an end.

Due to its central location and possession of necessary facilities, Pennsylvania became a logical meeting ground for general meetings of all of the colonies. The first such general meeting was the First Continental Congress that met in October of 1774 in Philadelphia's Carpenters' Hall, a building built by the Carpenter Company of the city and county of Philadelphia (a carpenters' guild). The result of the meeting was the *Declaration and Resolves of the First Continental Congress*, which stated that persons in the British colonies had not given up their British citizenship and had the same rights as those persons living in Britain.

Carpenters' Hall, Philadelphia

Thus, predominately due to its central location, the colony of Pennsylvania, and specifically the city of Philadelphia, quickly became known as the "cradle of independence" for the colonies.

COLONY DISPUTES

As the colony expanded, border disputes arose with neighboring colonies. These disputes took many years to resolve and in some cases resulted in armed conflicts between settlers. The main disputes were as follows:

Maryland
The charter for Maryland granted in 1632 by Charles I and the charter for Pennsylvania granted in 1681 by Charles II led to considerable argument between Lord Baltimore and William Penn. The Maryland charter would have included what is now Philadelphia, and the Pennsylvania charter included what is today the city of Baltimore, but much of the dispute focused on the area of (present-day) Delaware. Finally in 1760, Lord Baltimore

recognized Delaware as a separate entity and, as a boundary between Pennsylvania and Delaware, a twelve-mile arc was drawn with the courthouse in Newcastle as the center point (the only circular boundary in the United States). This did not completely settle the dispute. In 1763, the proprietors of Maryland and Pennsylvania agreed to hire surveyors to clearly mark the east/west border between the two states. Charles Mason, an English astronomer, and his assistant, Jeremiah Dixon, accepted the task. After four years of work, the result was a boundary marked by a line of stone markers placed at five-mile intervals. This unassuming border of stone markers became known as the famous Mason-Dixon Line and succeeded in settling territorial disputes between Maryland and Pennsylvania.

Virginia

The original Virginia charter granted the state all lands "running west and northwest up into the country from sea to sea." As the settlers moved to the west, the boundary of the southwestern area of the Pennsylvania colony came under dispute. Both Virginia and Pennsylvania claimed ownership of the area. The quarrel was further complicated in 1749, when the Ohio Company was formed and granted 500,000 acres—some of which lay in the area disputed between Virginia and Pennsylvania. In 1773, Penn petitioned the British parliament for a settlement, to no avail. The Virginia claim was so prevalent that from 1775 until 1780 Pittsburgh was virtually governed by Virginia. Finally, in 1779, the dispute was settled by extending the Mason-Dixon line 5 degrees of longitude west of Delaware and then due north to Lake Erie. The claims of settlers in this land granted by the state of Virginia were to be recognized by the state of Pennsylvania.

Connecticut

The original Connecticut Charter of 1662 granted Connecticut the territory west to the Pacific Ocean but accepted any territory "then possessed by other Christian princes or States." (The Charter of Pennsylvania was granted in 1681.) Little interest was shown for this area until 1750, when the Wyoming Valley was discovered by a

Connecticut explorer. This led to the establishment of the Susquehanna Company, a private company in Connecticut that undertook the settlement of the valley. In 1762, two hundred settlers from Connecticut entered the valley, only to be met by hostile Indians. After an Indian attack in which twenty settlers were scalped, the settlers retreated back to Connecticut. Slowly, over time, settlers from Pennsylvania entered the valley, and in 1763 Penn petitioned the court to halt settlers from Connecticut from entering the area. The court so ruled, but it did little to stem the influx from Connecticut. In 1764, Penn signed a treaty with the Indians at Fort Stanwix whereby he once again bought the area from the Indians. This thereby voided Connecticut's claim to the area.

Both colonies continued settling the region, and finally in 1769 conflict arose between the settlers of the two states. These clashes were known as the Pennamite Wars, which erupted sporadically between 1769 and 1775. The Connecticut settlers were expelled from the area on five separate occasions, but they kept returning.

The dispute continued until 1782, when a special court agreed with Penn's claim to the area in what came to be known as the Trenton Decree. The decree stated that the land held by the Connecticut settlers should be recognized as legal and that Pennsylvania settlers with claims to the same land should receive money in lieu of the land. This finally ended the long dispute between the two states.

People

Initially, the population of the Penn colony was predominately English Quakers, but when Penn returned to England in 1692, he began a process of recruiting potential settlers from other areas where they may have been suffering religious persecution. This effort led to an increase of other religious groups arriving in the colony. For example, German reformists, including the Mennonites, came in droves (from 1749 to 1754 at the rate of about five thousand per year), settling in the Lancaster area. Today they are known as the "Pennsylvania Dutch." They tended to live among themselves and to continue their religious beliefs, their distinctive art forms, their language, and their way of life. Pennsylvania continued to be tolerant of such subcultures.

By the middle of the eighteenth century, almost one-third of the state's population was German and German-speaking. They were soon joined by Anglicans from England as well as Irish Catholics and Welsh. The first Catholic congregation in the state was organized in 1720, and by the end of the colonial period, Pennsylvania had the second largest Catholic population among all the colonies.

Many of those who arrived in America came as indentured servants— almost one-third of all of the early immigrants to Pennsylvania were indentured. They consisted predominately of young men who accepted an indenture of three to seven years as a payment to finance their passage to the New World. Another group of servant-class immigrants were African Americans. By 1730, four thousand Africans had been imported into the state as slaves. The importation of slaves was a constant source of conflict for the early settlers. The very first abolitionist petition in American history was written by four Quaker men in 1688. Those men, Garret Hendricks, Derick O. de'Graeft, Francis Danniell Pastorious, and Abraham Op den Graef, presented it at the Quaker yearly meeting, but it was not acted on by the assembly. The 1750 census for Philadelphia shows an indentured servant population of 1,479 and a slave population of 787.

As a further indication of the settlers' views on African Americans, one can look at the question of marriage for slaves. Marriages between slaves were not recognized (even if married in a church). In addition, after 1725, interracial marriages were banned. The white participant could be sold as a servant for seven years, free Negroes were enslaved, and the children of such marriages were sold into slavery for 31 years.

Being a Quaker colony, the people of Pennsylvania were pacifists by nature, which had a great impact on the early development of the colony. France, Canada, and Virginia all claimed possession of the Ohio Valley. The French built forts to protect their claims to include Fort Duquesne in the area of present-day Pittsburgh. In 1754, when George Washington led a force into the Ohio Valley, his troops were comprised of Virginians, not Pennsylvanians, and the same was true in 1755 when General Braddock captured Fort Duquesne. There were no Pennsylvanians among his troops. Pennsylvania was still a pacifist colony.

In 1756, when the Indian raids became extensive, Pennsylvania changed its pacifist course and that year established forty forts from the Delaware Water Gap over the Blue Mountains into the Juniata Valley. And in 1758, Pennsylvania contributed 2,700 volunteers and four battalions of Royal Americans to the British Army to counter the French activity in the northern part of the colony. The Quaker influence was waning out of necessity for survival.

ECONOMY

The early economy of Pennsylvania was centered on agriculture, predominately for subsistence, and furs for exportation to Europe— beaver fur was extremely fashionable at the time. Later, as the farmer became more proficient and attuned to the Pennsylvanian soil, Pennsylvania became known as the "Bread Basket of the British Empire." Flour processed by the flour mills throughout the colony was shipped not only to other colonies but in vast amounts to Europe and the Caribbean.

In 1765, the Penn family permitted York County farmers to exhibit their produce. The charter signed by Thomas Penn, son of William Penn, granted York the privilege of "forever hereafter" holding two fairs a year, one in spring and one in the fall. The York Fair was discontinued in 1815 at citizens' request due to rioting and the murder of Robert Dunn at the fair. In 1853 the fair again reopened, sponsored by the newly formed York County Agricultural Society. It has continued to this day.

From the onset of the colony, William Penn was aware that roads would be required to move the produce from the farms to the towns and cities. As early as July of 1681, William Penn stipulated that "Great roads from City to City not to contain less than forty feet in breadth shall be first laid out and declared to be highways. . . ." Later, in 1689, the council passed an act stating that "the justices of the county courts could provide for the laying out of land roads or cartways, but all king's highways or public roads were to be laid out upon orders from the governor and Council."

At the same time, manufacturing was making great inroads for the economy of the state. Iron forges were prevalent in many areas along with flour mills. Artisans began small independent industries to meet the various needs of the settlers. Shoemakers, saddle makers, furniture factories, as well as other manufacturing venues began to appear throughout the state. For example, in 1751 Lancaster, the first inland town of any size in British America, had over 350 artisans working along with eight-seven wagon makers, fifty-nine merchants and shopkeepers, and twenty lawyers and doctors. Some early inventions included the Conestoga wagon, which could carry up to four tons of cargo, and Ben Franklin's "Pennsylvania fireplace" or "Franklin stove." Along the coastal areas, shipbuilding became one of the major industries: aimed at further enhancing the capability of the merchants to ship their products not only to Britain but to other customers in Europe as well.

Coal, later to become a major industry in Pennsylvania, was first discovered in the state around 1751, when John Pattin reported the finding of bituminous coal along the Kiskiminetas River near Salisburg. Later, between 1750 and 1755, an Indian gave anthracite coal, known as "stone coal," to a gunsmith in Nazareth, Pennsylvania, for repairing his rifle. By 1761, the first recorded coal mine was operating in Pennsylvania on Coal Hill (now Mount Washington) across the Monongahela River from Fort Pitt. About the same time, Wyoming Valley was using coal for heating, and by 1768, a survey of Wyoming Valley noted "stone coal" near the mouth of Toby's Creek. The year 1766 saw the first recorded mine fire in Pennsylvania at the Coal Hill mine. And by 1769, a blacksmith by the name of Obadiah Gore was using coal in his blacksmith forge in lieu of charcoal. Along with the discovery of coal deposits, early settlers were also reporting the finding of mines for pewter, lead, and copper, but it would be years before these mining industries blossomed.

One anomaly of the Quaker society was the manufacturing of a long rifle that came to be known as the Pennsylvania long rifle. Early in the 1700s, German and Swiss immigrants arrived with knowledge of the manufacturing of firearms. They had been producing them since the late 1600s. Unlike the British muskets of the period, the Germans produced a rifled weapon that became very popular.

The main center for the production of the Pennsylvania long rifle was Lancaster. This rifle later became known as the Kentucky rifle because of the feats of Daniel Boone and other early settlers that settled in the land that became Kentucky. The industry that started in Lancaster soon spread to Berks, Lebanon, Lehigh, Northampton, Snyder, and Union counties as well as the entire Cumberland Valley. In Lancaster, the name Martin Meylin is associated with the early manufacturing of the rifle, although there is no definite proof he ever produced a rifle.

Philadelphia was rapidly becoming one of the most important centers for foreign trade on the Eastern Seaboard. In the 1750s, the city of Philadelphia was the second-largest English-speaking city in the world, second only to London. Its economic base served as an incentive to create the necessary services for its citizens. By 1751, Philadelphia had America's first hospital, known as the Pennsylvania Hospital. It was founded by Benjamin Franklin and Dr. Thomas Bond.

Pennsylvania's economy was varied, thereby providing a strong independent base for the colony. It also created problems, as the three distinct economic interest groups—the agriculturists, the artisans, and later the manufacturing elements—were often not in harmony with the colonial government. Each element became very protective of their rights and privileges, often causing serious friction between the various classes as well as the state government. Friction arose when England, in 1750, tried to dictate that the colony of Pennsylvania would trade only with England and her colonies.

Arts and Culture

The growth of Philadelphia not only encompassed the people and the economic strength of the city, but it turned the city into one of the cultural centers of the British colonies in America. Philadelphia soon became known as the "Athens of America" for the ideas that were flowing from its intellectuals. Penn's idea of freedom of expression made it conducive to a "thinking society." "The Junto," initially formed as a working man's organization for the discussion of ideas, soon became the American Philosophical Society, with such famous members as Benjamin Franklin, David Rittenhouse, John Bartram, and Benjamin West. These men wrote at great length regarding their experiments, findings, and thoughts. In 1733, Benjamin Franklin began publishing *Poor Richard's Almanac* under the assumed name of Richard Sanders.

In the area of advances in medicine, the medical community in Philadelphia was one of the more advanced in the colonies. When Lady Mary Worley Montaque, the wife of the British ambassador to Turkey, reported that the Turks were immunizing patients by causing slight cases of smallpox (now known as inoculation), the Philadelphia physicians were quick to experiment with the treatment. This was well before Dr. Edward Jenner wrote his famous paper on smallpox inoculation in 1798.

In 1740, Philadelphia opened "The Academy," which by 1755 had become the College of Philadelphia: the first nondenominational college in the British colonies. Today it is known as the University of Pennsylvania.

With the Quaker condemnation of slavery in Pennsylvania, an African American subculture began to emerge around 1758, especially in large towns such as Philadelphia. Again following the dictate of William Penn for religious freedom, African American churches began to spring up, making Pennsylvania the first state to openly promote religious and ethnic diversity.

Benjamin Franklin was a moving force in Philadelphia during this period. Due mainly to his urging, the streets of Philadelphia were paved, cleaned, and illuminated. He also established fire companies, a fire insurance company, and the first circulating library in the colonies.

The German settlers in Pennsylvania had their own unique art forms that they brought with them from Europe. They soon introduced

Examples of early Pennsylvania Dutch pottery.

what became known as "red pottery," a form of pottery decorated with a base color of red and various bright colors in additional decoration, a form similar to that of German pottery.

In addition, they also continued their European tradition of creating "frakturs," an art form that commemorates an important event, such as a birth, wedding, etc. Frakturs were illuminated manuscripts decorated with various significant decorative symbols around the edges, with the center of the document containing the story of the event commemorated. The word *fraktur* arose as the description of a specific typeface used for printing—the fractured look.

An early fraktur.

Rosette hex sign

The Pennsylvania Dutch tradition of decorating barns with what became known as hex signs did not appear until around the early 1830s, as the cost of paint in the earlier period was too prohibitive to allow for such decoration. While there is no definite explanation as to why they are called hex signs, the various symbols used, such as a heart for love, do give meaning to the signs. As an example, the hex sign, known as the rosette, contains a center of a single rosette—a symbol for good luck—and a scalloped border symbolizing smooth sailing. The two colors used are red, signifying strength, and green, symbolic of life.

THE INDIANS

From the very beginning, William Penn made great efforts to be friendly with the local Indian tribes. As early as 1683, he met with a Delaware Indian chief known as Tammany, and a mutual respect developed between the two men. This respect can be shown by a Tammany quote: "We will live in peace with Onas (Penn) and his children as long as the sun and moon shall endure."

As more and more settlers arrived in Pennsylvania in search of land, William Penn's dictum that all land acquired from the Indians must be purchased or accomplished by the signing of a treaty proved difficult and restricting. In the 1730s, William Penn's son, anxious to acquire new land, discovered an old unsigned draft treaty from 1686 and decided to use it as a basis for acquisition of new land. The treaty, never implemented, would have allowed for the acquisition of Lenape land north of the Delaware River in a unique way. The treaty stated that a man could acquire all the land as far as he could walk in a day and a half. In 1737, the Penn brothers convinced four Delaware chieftains of the validity of the treaty, and a walk began on September 19. Three men started the walk, but only one, Edward Marshall, completed it. The other two gave up the challenge. His endeavors added 750,000 acres to the Penn holdings. The Lenape Indians, however, did not want to leave their land, which led to a conference in Philadelphia in 1742 attended by several Iroquois chieftains. After receiving various gifts from the settlers, the chieftains ordered the Lenape (Delawares) off the land acquired through the walking purchase. This marks the beginning of the troubles between the Indians and settlers in Pennsylvania.

Another important land purchase was via the Treaty of Lancaster in 1744, whereby the Six Nations ceded all their land to the "setting sun," meaning to the western edge of the Allegheny Mountains. By the mid 1700s, all the good farmland had been purchased by the colonists leaving the native tribes with few choices but to move to other areas. And finally, the Albany Land Purchase of 1754 put the Indians on a war footing. That land purchase, negotiated by Penn's representatives at the Iroquois Albany Congress, secured a deed to all the land on a line from Shamokin to Lake Erie and extending to the extreme southern limits of the province. The Indians, in effect, were forced to move their homes west of the Ohio River, where they soon joined forces with the French.

The early Indian wars were basically tribe against tribe and usually over territorial disputes. However, over time the continual loss of land and privileges led the tribes to turn against the settlers. The semi-peaceful atmosphere that existed between the Indians and the settlers of Pennsylvania was shattered on October 17, 1755, when Indians initiated their first attack on settlers east of the Alleghenies. The attack took place at Penn's Creek, in the western part of the state. Along with the attacks came the Indian practice of taking captives in the raids. The captives were usually young persons and most frequently female. For example, Mary Jemison from the Buchanan Valley in Adams County and the sisters Sara and Rhonda Boyd from the western part of the state were early captives.

In 1754, many Indian tribes allied themselves with the French against the British in what became known as the French and Indian War. A treaty signed in Easton, Pennsylvania, in 1758 ended the war. However, it was followed by what is known as Pontiac's Rebellion in

1763. Pontiac's Rebellion occurred when the Treaty of Easton, signed between the Indian tribes of the Ohio Valley and Pennsylvania, was violated by the settlers. The treaty had guaranteed no settlements west of the Appalachian Mountains, and in return the Indians agreed not to fight with the French against the British. As soon as settlements began appearing west of the Appalachians, the Indian chief Pontiac launched bloody attacks. Many atrocities occurred on both sides of the conflict. Finally, in 1763, Colonel Henry Bouquet defeated the Indians in western Pennsylvania in the Battle of Bushy Run and then retook Fort Pitt from the Indians, thus marking the beginning of the end of French domination in western Pennsylvania.

The French and Indian War, followed by the bloody Pontiac Rebellion atrocities, led to a feeling of genuine hatred against the Indians. Atrocities had occurred on both sides, but the Indians had shown the greater propensity for cruel treatment of captured settlers. An example of this anger was the Conestoga Massacre that occurred in Lancaster in December of 1763. At that time there were only about twenty Susquehannock Indians in the Lancaster area, all Christians. On December 14, 1763, a gang of ruffians known as the Paxton boys swept into the Conestoga camp, killing six of the residents. The fourteen who survived were placed under protective custody in the jail, only to have the jail overrun by the Paxton boys and all the Indians killed in the raid.

As part of the resulting treaty with the Indians signed in 1766 in Oswego, New York, Colonel Bouquet demanded that the various Indian tribes return their captives. In all, 306 captives were returned by the Indians, including Sara and Rhonda Boyd but not Mary Jemison. The returned captives were taken to Carlisle, where many were returned to their families. However, some had been away so long that they no longer remembered their families or even their family name. One captive, Mary Jemison, remained with the Seneca tribe for the remainder of her life, marrying and raising a family, and became known by the name Dehgewanus, meaning "two falling voices." She lived among the Indians for more than sixty years. In 1910, a statue of Mary Jemison was erected near the site of her abduction in Buchanan Valley.

Mary Jemison

Many of the English officers and men returning from the Bouquet expedition petitioned Penn for land in payment of their services. Penn decided the grants would be recognized only if additional land could be acquired from the Indians. A meeting was held at Fort Stanwix, near Rome, New York, in 1768, between Penn's representatives and the local Indians. The result was an agreement by the Indians to cede a large portion of land on the west branch of the Susquehanna River to the Penns for the payment of $10,000. The treaty was signed on November 5, 1768. Land grant claims presented a serious problem, however, as the Indians frequently sold the same piece of land to several purchasers.

During this period, pestilence and disease brought to the New World by the settlers continued to wreak havoc on the local Indian populations. Yellow fever, typhus, and smallpox epidemics were frequent occurrences among the Indian tribes. The settlers were known to supply the Indians with blankets thought to be infected with the yellow fever germs in hopes of infecting the Indians. The white man's presence was being felt not only in loss of land but in loss of Indian lives as well.

The Quaker period effectively ended when they lost control of the Pennsylvania Assembly and the colony due to the perceived necessity of shifting from a totally pacifistic society to one more aggressive in nature. William Penn's ideals had in fact served the colony well in its formative years, leading not only to a thriving and prosperous colony but also to the creation of Philadelphia, which became an intellectual center admired throughout the world. And while the Quaker ideals diminished in the later society, they have never been completely lost to this day.

Chapter Five

Birth of a State and a Nation
(1774–1800)

General History

The last twenty-six years of the eighteenth century were for Pennsylvania a very traumatic time, as they were for all of the colonies. Not only did the state have to deal with supporting a revolution against England but also with the establishment of a sovereign state within a confederation of states. The transition was made, but not without a fair amount of turmoil. Change did not come easy.

National

While Pennsylvania may have been slow to believe in total independence from Britain, citizens of the colony soon caught independence fever and joined wholeheartedly in the cause. And when a location was needed for the First Continental Congress, Pennsylvania came immediately to mind for several reasons. Pennsylvania had become one of the major colonies and just happened to be located geographically in the middle of the thirteen colonies—a necessity considering the rigors of travel in those early days. Philadelphia had also become the second largest city in the British Empire and a major center of culture and advancement in the colonies.

The First Continental Congress met in Carpenter's Hall in Philadelphia from September 5 through October 4, 1774. The goal of this congress was to express to the British parliament their dissatisfaction with the current state of control demonstrated by parliament over the colonies. Members from all colonies attended. This congress produced the *Declaration and Resolves*, also known as the *Declaration of Rights and Grievances*.

The British refusal to negotiate with the colonies in any manner led to a Second Continental Congress, also in Philadelphia, from May 10, 1775, until December 12, 1776. The congress began about a month after the Revolutionary War had actually started. This congress was convinced that independence was the only answer. A Committee of Five was selected to create a declaration to be sent to the British. That committee was initially composed of John Adams, Massachusetts; Roger Sherman, Connecticut; Benjamin Franklin, Pennsylvania; Robert Livingston, New York; and Thomas Jefferson, Virginia. Later, the noted Pennsylvanian John Dickinson was added as a member. He and Thomas Jefferson wrote what came to be known as the *Declaration of the Causes and Necessity of Taking Up Arms*. The document, issued on July 6, 1775, was to inform the British parliament of the feelings of all the colonies.

A year later in reaction to the non-response to the declaration, Thomas Jefferson, at the request of the Committee of Five, in his room in Philadelphia, drafted what today is known as *The Declaration of Independence*, which was adopted on July 4, 1776.

Due to the fact that both of the Continental Congresses had met in Philadelphia, that city was looked upon as the new capital city for the colonies—making it a specific target for the British forces when the Revolutionary War broke out. In 1776, when the fortunes of war were not in favor of the colonists and the British were approaching Philadelphia, the Continental Congress moved to the Henry Fife House in Baltimore, Maryland. As the tide began to turn in the spring of 1777, Congress returned to Philadelphia and remained there until September of that year. However, by September of 1777, Philadelphia was again threatened, and the Congress moved once more: first to Lancaster, Pennsylvania, where they met for one day on September 27, 1777, and then on to York, Pennsylvania, where they felt the broad Susquehanna River would protect them from the British. They remained in York from September 30, 1777, until June 27, 1778, during which time *The Articles of Confederation* were written. Congress once again returned to Philadelphia, where it remained until June of 1783, when it moved to Princeton, New Jersey, with subsequent

U.S. Capitol building in York, Pennsylvania.

OLD COURT-HOUSE AT LANCASTER, BUILT 1784-1787.

U. S. Capitol building in Lancaster, Pennsylvania.

47

moves to Annapolis, Maryland; Trenton, New Jersey; New York City; once again to Philadelphia from December 1790 to May 14, 1800; and finally to Washington, DC, on November 17, 1800. All in all, Pennsylvania had hosted the new nation's capital on eight different occasions.

The last major act of intercolonial importance held in Philadelphia was the Federal Constitutional Convention in late 1787, the convention that led to the creation of the United States Constitution. After much discussion, the final document was signed on September 17, 1787. Pennsylvania was the second state to ratify the document on December 12, 1787.

Due to the state of Pennsylvania's central location and the renown of the city of Philadelphia, the city became then and remains today the real focal point of the American Revolution. While Boston was the initial instigator of the revolution, the focus shifted quickly to Philadelphia where the Continental Congresses met and where the major documents of the American Revolution were created.

The Pennsylvanians involved in the early formation of the nation were nearly all from the Philadelphia area—men such as John Dickinson, James Wilson, Robert Morris, and Benjamin Franklin. Benjamin Franklin was already a famous man before the revolutionary fervor began; after all, he had invented the Franklin stove, published *Poor Richard's Almanac*, and invented not only the bifocal lens but the lightening rod as well. But he was also recognized for his diplomatic skills.

In 1757, Franklin was sent to England to represent the citizens of Pennsylvania in their efforts to wrest control of the state from the Penn family. He remained in England until 1775 and eventually represented not only Pennsylvania but the states of Georgia, New Jersey, and Massachusetts in their dealings with the Crown. His speech before the British parliament regarding the Stamp Act helped to persuade parliament to repeal the bill. Franklin was halfway across the Atlantic on his return to the colonies when the Revolutionary War began in 1775. After serving in the Second Continental Congress, Franklin was sent to Paris, where he negotiated a Treaty of Alliance with the French in 1778, and he was present at the Treaty of Paris that ended the American Revolutionary War. Benjamin Franklin was not only a great Pennsylvanian but also a great American patriot.

INTERNAL

The year 1774 was a critical one for the American colonies, especially for the colony of Massachusetts. That particular colony, in the eyes of the British, needed corrective actions—as their general obstreperous actions such as the Boston Tea Party could not be allowed to continue. This resulted in a series of acts by the British parliament known as the Coercive Acts by the British and as the Intolerable Acts by the colonists in Massachusetts. The acts, all aimed at regaining control of the Massachusetts colony, had little impact on the other colonies. Some of the colonies were totally supportive of colonists in Massachusetts, and some were less than enthusiastic about their cause.

Pennsylvanian's sentiments for their sister colony were, at best, lukewarm. In this state there continued to be a major chasm between the elite (the merchant class) and the working class. The elitists did not want to change the status quo—they were doing quite well under the current conditions. This resistance to change, which was predominately in Philadelphia, reached center stage when Governor John Penn refused to summon the assembly to select delegates to the First Continental Congress. The goal of the Congress was to create a joint response to the Coercive Acts passed by Parliament. Penn saw no need for such action.

A major chasm existed, however, between the elite merchant class and the Pennsylvania settlers outside of Philadelphia and the working class within the city, the majority of whom opposed the acts and took matters into their own hands. They formed Committees of Correspondence, who elected delegates from Pennsylvania to the Continental Congress. Thus began the demise of the assembly form of government for Pennsylvania.

After the September 1774 meeting of the Continental Congress, Pennsylvania radicals began a concerted effort to overthrow the colony's provisional government.

To further encourage the radicals, the Continental Congress turned down the assembly's offer to meet in their chambers (now known as Independence Hall) and instead accepted the offer to meet in Carpenters' Hall, as that location "was highly agreeable to the mechanics and citizens in general, but mortifying in the last degree to Joseph Galloway." Joseph Galloway was the long-time Speaker of the Pennsylvania Assembly and an avowed Tory.

The situation became more intense when the Continental Congress authorized the extralegal Committees of Associators that were rapidly forming in the state to enforce the Continental Association requirement to boycott commerce with Britain. The merchants of Philadelphia did not want this—it was too much of a loss of income for them to accede. Finally, in May of 1775, when the Revolutionary War broke out in Massachusetts, the Pennsylvania Assembly and the proprietors in Philadelphia refused to act on behalf of their fellow colonies.

Here again, the Associators rapidly organized a militia system, sponsored by the Committee of Privates, to send troops to fight with the Continental Army. Troops from Lancaster, Berks, and York counties were sent north to assist the Continental Army. All of this was without direct authority from the state assembly, which, like the city of Philadelphia, continued to resist the revolution. The wealthy were satisfied with the status quo, as they continued to increase their wealth.

Ultimately, it took the Continental Congress's recommendation of May 10, 1776—to install state governments in lieu of the colonial governments—to overthrow the Pennsylvania Assembly and create a new, pro-revolutionary government. One of the prime moving forces in this effort was Thomas Paine's tract "Common Sense" published in 1776.

The finale for the assembly came in May of 1776, when the leader of the Committee of Privates, James Cannon, declared that the Pennsylvania Assembly, "having abdicated the government, and by their acts of detestable cowardice had laid the Provincial Conference under the necessity of taking instant charge of affair." Calling for a convention in June, the assembly was dissolved. To be eligible as a representative to the conference one had to repudiate allegiance to the Crown and swear that they believed in the Holy Trinity. Since early Quakers denied the Holy Spirit, these restrictions effectively eliminated most of the Quakers and much of the population in the three oldest counties from eligibility in the new government. The new "eligibles" would write the first Pennsylvania constitution. Faced with this reality, the Pennsylvania Assembly (which opposed the revolution to the very end) went out of business in the fall of 1776.

The rise of a new form of government caused many changes in the political system of the state. The Quakers forced out the "fighting Quakers" who had taken up arms against the British. Simultaneously, two new political parties arose—the Radicals, or Constitution Party, who implemented a revolutionary state government, and the moderates, known as the Republicans, who opposed the new government. Particularly repulsive to the Republicans were the Radicals' efforts to redistribute power down the social ladder and to the western parts of the state.

The distribution of the seats in the assembly became a very contentious point between the western and eastern parts of the state. In 1764, with eight counties in existence, the three eastern counties of Chester, Philadelphia, and Bucks held twenty of the thirty-six seats in the colonial assembly. In 1776, the new state assembly increased the ratio to thirty for the three counties and twenty-eight for the remaining counties, thereby recognizing the increased population in the outlaying counties.

The new state government was established to govern until the new constitution was completed and Committees of Associators were formed to enforce the edicts of the new state assembly. These committees kept Washington and his troops supplied with food, clothing, and munitions, particularly during the time he and his army spent at Valley Forge.

The first constitution for the state of Pennsylvania was passed on September 28, 1776. It contained provisions allowing taxpayers (including African Americans) and their sons over the age of twenty-one the right to vote, it expanded representation to the western areas of the state, and it established a single-house legislature as well as a supreme executive council in lieu of a governor. The constitution included a section entitled Declaration of Rights that contained twenty-eight specific articles detailing the individual rights of Pennsylvania citizens. It is important to note that all of the later constitutions for the state of Pennsylvania contain the section titled Declaration of Rights as stated in the first constitution. It also required taking a "test oath" affirming in the presence of God loyalty to the constitution, thus disenfranchising many Quakers, Loyalists, and neutrals, who would not sign the oath, as while they believed in God he was not a central figure one swore to. One of the major stumbling blocks for the new government was that any new proposed law had to be taken back to a representative's constituency for local approval and then returned to the next annual session of the assembly for passage.

The constitution was opposed by many of the early leaders of the state, including John Dickinson, James Wilson, Robert Morris, and Frederick Muhlenberg, who disliked the emphasis of "inclusion" of all classes and areas. However, the constitution was adopted and the Constitution Party, or Radicals, led by Joseph Reed, George Bryan, and William Findley, prevailed. They governed the state until 1790, when a new revised constitution was written and adopted. One of the early initiatives of the new government occurred in 1779, when an act was passed that took ownership of all the public land owned by the Penn family (with compensation). Another of the major accomplishments of the Constitution Party was an act in 1780 that called for the gradual abolition of slavery. The African American slave population dropped from 3,737 in 1790 to 64 by 1840, and by 1850, all African American slaves in Pennsylvania were free except for those who had escaped from the South. The escaping slaves were protected by local abolitionist groups. Pennsylvania was the first state to officially abolish slavery.

The new government's financial policies soon ran into difficulties. Inflation was rampant, causing severe monetary hardships—particularly on working-class individuals. Many began to resent the wealthy merchant class, who not only appeared insulated against inflation but also avoided military service. Tempers finally erupted on October 4, 1779, when rioters attacked the home of James Wilson, a signer of the

Declaration of Independence. He was not only a member of the elite wealthy class but had defended the Loyalists in Philadelphia who had worked with the British during the occupation.

Additionally, the question of financial remuneration to the Penn family for their land grant arose. The Divesting Act of 1779 deprived the Penn family of their ownership in payment of the amount of 120,000 pounds sterling. That amount was to be paid in increments of 15 to 20,000 pounds yearly. Finally, on April 9, 1791, the state legislature passed a bill to pay the total amount in one payment. The Penn family also received from the British government a yearly payment of 4,000 pounds, and this payment continued for over one hundred years.

Ultimately, in 1789, it was decided to rewrite the state constitution. An assembly was held in November, and the resulting constitution was a merger between the radicals and the conservatives. The new constitution retained the Declaration of Rights segment of the previous constitution but made some radical changes in the organization of the state government. The 1789 constitution called for a second legislative house to be known as the Senate, a strong governor who replaced the Supreme Executive Council of the previous constitution, and state judges appointed by the governor.

While the state government appeared to be generally accepted by the population of the state, the distinction between the wealthy merchant class and the working classes remained strong, as did the distinction between the citizens of the state in the eastern areas and those from the more recently settled western areas of the state.

In a move to better unite the various interests of the state, the state capital moved from Philadelphia to Lancaster in 1799. It remained there until 1810, when it moved to Harrisburg—a more central location.

As the new nation began to emerge, Pennsylvania, along with the other colonies, had its share of assimilation problems. From 1790 until 1800, Philadelphia served as the capital of the new nation, and consequently the citizens of Philadelphia were probably the best informed citizens in the new country. George Washington, the first president, and his Federalist Party, initially had the support of the citizens of the state, but as time went by, many citizens became concerned about the aristocratic nature of the party. This was a problem that had plagued

Pennsylvania for years—the divide between the aristocrat and the working class. The eastern part of the state appeared to be settling into its new role as a member of a larger governmental structure, but the western part remained very skeptical and obstructive.

Western Pennsylvanians remained concerned about the values of the federal government. They were still being attacked by hostile Indians and received little protection from the new government. In addition, taxation was a major issue. One of the actions taken by the new federal government was to assume the state debts that had occurred as a result of the Revolutionary War. Payment of the debts required an influx of funds. To this end, Alexander Hamilton proposed and enacted an excise tax on whiskey amounting to about 25 percent. This tax was very harmful to the western part of Pennsylvania, where most of the whiskey was made. They refused to pay the tax. When the new federal government went to the governor of Pennsylvania, Thomas Mifflin, he refused to put down the insurrection. Further, Pennsylvania Supreme Court Justice McKean refused the federal government the power to use force to end the insurrection. The new country's first constitutional crisis had arisen.

Finally, in the summer of 1794, fighting had broken out in the Bedford area, and military action was required. President Washington, back in uniform, called for thirteen thousand troops to assemble at Carlisle to be employed to end the insurrection. This army became known as the "Watermelon Army" as provisions were short for the army and they stole from the local farmers—often watermelons. The army moved west as far as Bedford, and the insurrection was quelled.

Conflict between the federal government and the citizens of Pennsylvania arose again in 1798—once again over the issue of the federal levying of taxes on the state. The United States needed finances in case of a war with France, and a tax levy was placed on each state. The tax was levied for "evaluation of lands and dwelling houses and the enumeration of slaves" and since Pennsylvania had few slaves, it fell predominately on houses. Of the national $2 million amount, Pennsylvania was assessed $237,177.72. The German population in the eastern part of the state reacted adversely and an insurrection arose, lead by John Fries. Eventually, President John Adams ordered the rioters to disperse and requested the governor to use the militia to subdue the rioters. John Fries was captured and tried for treason, found guilty, and then pardoned, ending the rebellion.

The Whiskey Rebellion, and the later Fries Rebellion, as they became known, were major milestones for the new federal government. It was an issue of states' rights over federal rights, and Washington's action reinforced the founding fathers' concepts of federal rights. The ending of the Whiskey Rebellion did not go unnoticed by the other colonies, and a true unification of the country took a major step forward as a result of the action.

MILITARY

The male residents of Pennsylvania did not all share a desire to serve in the military to protect their state. By far the largest contingent of troops came from the Scotch/Irish segment of the population. They represented almost one-third of all the military from Pennsylvania in the Revolutionary War. In all, Pennsylvania supplied about 35,000 militia troops, 14 line regiments commanded by General Wayne under George Washington, and a small naval force of about 27 craft and 768 men. The main mission of the navy was to protect Philadelphia. The forces did themselves proud during the entire war period. But not all Pennsylvanians fought on the side of the colonies. Male citizens of Philadelphia provided two regiments for the British Army.

Once the Revolutionary War began in earnest, the British strategy immediately focused on taking Philadelphia. After all, it was the capital of this new upstart country, and European military strategy dictated that an army should give a high priority to the capture of the enemy capital. Such a capture may well precipitate the collapse of the enemy's cause. They also looked upon Philadelphia as a loyalist stronghold and felt if the British controlled the city they would no doubt recruit many loyalist followers into the British Army.

The colony of Pennsylvania had its first brush with the military actions of the war in the late fall of 1776, when General Washington and his troops retreated to Pennsylvania with the British forces in pursuit. The troops encamped along the Pennsylvania shores of the Delaware River, regrouping and planning. On Christmas Eve, General Washington and his troops crossed the partially frozen Delaware River at McCaskey's Ferry and surprised the Hessian troops in Trenton, New Jersey. They took many Hessian prisoners and retreated once again back into Pennsylvania. This was followed by Washington's military actions in New Jersey, which included the battles at Monmouth and Princeton—Pennsylvania had again escaped military action.

Then in mid-1777, the British developed a plan that called for General Burgoyne to launch a campaign to enter New York from Canada—commencing on June 17, 1777, with the goal of cutting off New England from the other colonies. Meanwhile, General Howe, on July 23, 1777, decided to undertake the capture of Philadelphia in lieu of joining General Burgoyne in New York. Howe's troops sailed up the Chesapeake Bay, disembarking at the head of the Elk River. For the first time in the Revolutionary War, Pennsylvania was about to feel the full impact of the war. As Howe moved south, so did General Washington, who rapidly moved his troops overland into Pennsylvania.

The first encounter between the British and American forces in Pennsylvania took place at Brandywine on September 11, 1777. Washington had deployed his troops at strategic locations along the Brandywine River—those locations that had fords for crossing the river. He also had his troops remove all boats along the river that could be used for the crossing of troops. In the ensuing battle, the revolutionary forces were defeated and forced to retreat. The colonial army retreated to Chester, Philadelphia, and Germantown to regroup.

On September 15, Washington advanced his troops to Warren Tavern on the Lancaster Pike, but a heavy storm ruined the ammunition and he was forced to retreat to Yellow Springs and soon across the Schuykill River to Phoenixville. As Howe continued his advance, General Wayne operated in the rear area of the advancing British army—but his troops were surprised by the British on September 20 and 21 at Paoli with the result that many colonial troops were bayoneted. This battle became known as the Paoli Massacre.

Howe's troops continued on their way to Philadelphia, and on September 27 they entered the city, leaving a strong British force in Germantown. General Washington decided to attack the British force in Germantown using a four-prong attack. His attack, which might have succeeded, was hampered by dense fog, which led to mass confusion, and his army was required to retreat to White Marsh, about six miles north of Chestnut Hill.

Howe's army arrived in Philadelphia, but the twenty ships carrying supplies for his troops were still south of the city on the Delaware River. The obstacles in the way were Fort Mifflin on Mud Island south of Philadelphia, and Fort Mercer, near Mercer, New Jersey. The colonial army had strongly fortified these two forts, and their presence prevented the British ships from reaching Philadelphia. Finally, on November 10, the forts fell and the British ships could proceed. However, the fort defenses had served their purpose. Their obstinate refusal to surrender had given General Washington and his army time to move from White Marsh through Gulf Mills to Valley Forge, where he established his winter quarters.

Valley Forge, only about thirty-five miles from the British forces in Philadelphia, proved to be more than just winter quarters for the army. Their presence blocked the British forces from the rural areas near the city and thus prevented the British Army from obtaining

Washington's headquarters, Valley Forge

Troop quarters at Valley Forge.

Interior of quarters.

much needed food supplies for their troops. However, the stay was not an easy one. The accommodations were stark, the weather was bad, sickness was rampant, and morale was low.

In mid-June of 1778, General Clinton, who had replaced General Howe, fearing a French blockade, decided to withdraw from Philadelphia—it had not proved to be the Loyalist stronghold it was previously believed to be. Immediately after his departure, the Continental army reentered the city, and the military aspects of the Revolutionary War left Pennsylvania. By June 19, General Washington and his troops were once again on the move to follow General Clinton as he moved to New York.

As the war dragged on, the troops became discontented, particularly regarding pay and rations. On May 26, 1780, two Continental regiments marched through their camp in Morristown, New Jersey, demanding immediate payment of overdue salaries and full rations. The rebellion was ended by troops from Pennsylvania. On January 3, 1781, troops from Pennsylvania set up their own camp near Princeton, New Jersey, and chose their own representatives to negotiate with Pennsylvania state officials regarding their status, pay, and rations. A negotiated settlement was achieved, but over half of the mutineers abandoned the army in protest.

Throughout the period of military activity in Pennsylvania, there were major military hospitals in both Bethlehem and Lititz to take care of the wounded soldiers.

In addition to the British/American troops in battle, there was another active military arena during the 1770s—that of the frontier settlers. There were frequent raids on western Pennsylvania settlers by Indians, often inspired by British Loyalists. The most notorious of the raids took place in the Wyoming Valley near Wilkes Barre. The Wyoming Valley had been contested between Connecticut and Pennsylvania for many years and had resulted in the Pennamite-Yankee wars of 1769–1771 and again in 1775. The bad feeling arose again in 1778. The Loyalists and Indians saw an opportunity to retake the valley as many of the male settlers had joined the Continental army, leaving the valley poorly protected. A group led by John Butler along with Indian allies raided the valley on July 3, 1778. The settlers sought refuge in Forty Fort near Wilkes Barre but were soon defeated with major casualties. Such raids continued well into 1782, when on August 25, 1782, the Mohawk chief Joseph Brant conducted raids on settlements in Pennsylvania. Finally, on November 10, the Americans conducted a retaliatory raid against the Loyalists and Indians in the Ohio territory in the last battle of the Revolutionary War.

INDUSTRY

The Revolutionary War period did not slow down the growth of industry and innovation in the new state of Pennsylvania. Not only was the state flourishing in manufacturing but also it had become one of the true "bread baskets" for the nation. During the wartime period, Pennsylvania was a major supplier to the Continental army. In Carlisle, there was a major ordinance facility that produced cannons, muskets, and other armaments for the use of the army. A cottage industry for musketry was born as well, and a woman musket maker—a rarity—by the name of Catherine Smith emerged, making musket barrels for the Continental army.

Inventors also were busy at work. The technology level of the workers in Pennsylvania was so respected in Europe that when a Frenchman named Jean Louis Blanchard brought the first balloon to America for demonstration in December of 1792, he picked Philadelphia as the site of the flight. But flight was not the only means of transportation being experimented within Pennsylvania. On August 12, 1787, John Fitch had the first voyage of his steam-powered ship on the Delaware River (twenty years before Robert Fulton and the Claremont voyage). Fitch's steamboat was so successful that by 1790 his boats had a regular route between Philadelphia, Burlington, and Trenton, New Jersey.

Manufacturing was growing and in 1787, Tench Coxe established the Society for the Encouragement of Manufacturing. The function of this society was to encourage local manufacturing that would be beneficial to the new states. They pushed for the establishment of facilities in Pennsylvania to take the cotton from the southern states and turn it into textile, thereby avoiding shipping the cotton to England.

By 1800, Pennsylvania had become an industrial leader. It led its sister states in the production of textile, metal working, carpentry, and leather goods. While much of the work was done in cottage industries, the move was already underway to create major manufacturing facilities in the state. However, coal production, an area now synonymous with Pennsylvania, was not yet on the scene.

As early as 1766, Indians reported to the governor of Pennsylvania on the presence of coal deposits in Wyoming County, which was verified in 1779 by General Sullivan, who spoke of deposits of coal, lead, and copper. Nothing came of the report. Finally, in 1791, Philip Ginter reported his discovery of coal to Colonel Jacob Weiss, and the Lehigh Coal and Navigation Company was formed. However, the real coal industry did not begin until early in the nineteenth century.

To make manufacturing functional, good roads were required, and in 1792, the Philadelphia and Lancaster Turnpike Company was formed. This company created the first turnpike in America when they connected Philadelphia with Lancaster, a distance of sixty-five miles. It was the first paved road of its kind. Along with the movement of manufactured goods, transportation was required for the movement of citizens as well. In 1756, a stagecoach line was opened between Philadelphia and New York, followed in 1765 by coach service between Philadelphia and Baltimore.

However, along with the growth of manufacturing in the state, labor issues were also appearing. Abuse of workers finally led to the first strike in America in 1786. It was called by the Franklin Typographical Society and occurred over wages, with the printers refusing to work for less than six dollars a day. Later in 1795, the cabinetmakers issued a *Book of Prices* in an effort to protect their wages. The situation came to a head in 1805 when the shoemakers in Philadelphia went on strike. The state supreme court ruled that worker's organizations were unconstitutional conspiracies devaluing the owner's property and therefore engaged in theft. Thus began the long history of labor issues that have plagued Pennsylvania.

As industry began to develop so did the banking system. The Bank of North America was founded in Pennsylvania on May 26, 1787, and became an independent bank in 1790. It is the oldest bank in America. Later, in the early days of the state government, it was decided to form a Bank of Pennsylvania. Funds were needed to establish the endeavor, so Robert Morris, a Philadelphia merchant, convinced ninety-two patriots to provide 300,000 pounds sterling, and the bank was born. It was the first bank to be independently established in the new nation. Also in the financial arena, Pennsylvania has the distinction of establishing the first stock exchange in the United States. It was located in the City Tavern (soon to be renamed the Merchants Coffee House) in Philadelphia. The stock exchange building was destroyed by fire in 1834. The first insurance company to function in America was also established during this period.

PEOPLE

The population growth of the state of Pennsylvania during this period was, as census figures show, rapid: 200,000 persons in 1760; at least 300,000 persons in 1776. By 1790, that number had grown to 434,373 persons, of whom 211,000 lived in the seven most eastern counties: Chester, Philadelphia, Bucks, Lancaster, Berks, York, and Delaware. The remaining population was spread out over the remaining territory of the state.

As the population continued to grow, the cost of land increased as well. In 1762, land was priced at fifteen pounds plus two shillings quitrent (rent) per hundred acres. By 1765, with most of the good land already purchased, the cost was reduced to five pounds per hundred acres plus a quitrent of one penny. The quitrent was a vestige of the feudal era opposed by the settlers and therefore difficult to collect. The vast majority of the laboring class was in fact composed of indentured servants. The terms of service ranged from two to seven years—the vast majority being for a four- or five-year term. The varied nationalities of the indentured servants added a new diversity, both in ethnicity as well as religion.

During the Revolutionary War period, the population of Pennsylvania was not totally cohesive. Tensions were high, and in 1777 a Test Act was passed that stated if a person did not swear an oath of loyalty to the state of Pennsylvania and support of the revolution he would lose his citizen's rights. There were the ongoing factions such as Quakers versus non-Quakers, Elitists versus the general population, Loyalists versus Revolutionaries, Federalists versus anti-Federalists, and settlers in the western part of the state versus the population in the more urban areas. Each faction had its individual impact on the events of the time period. At least sixty estates were taken from Loyalist Pennsylvanians in retaliation for their allegiance to the British Crown.

Perhaps the newest factional conflict to emerge came with the expansion into the western part of the state. As the settlers moved farther and farther to the west they became more of a problem for the state government in Philadelphia. Such issues as protection from Indians, land purchases delayed in enactment of laws, and the judicial system, which remained centralized in Philadelphia, all gave rise to pressures from the western settlers to tend to their needs as well as those of the eastern part of the state. The issue was not settled until the post-Revolutionary period, and even then it remained festering for many years.

And while Pennsylvania was a "peace loving" colony due to its early Quaker background, by the time of the Revolutionary War, the city of Philadelphia had one of the highest crime rates in the colonies. The major offenses were assaults, burglary, and disorderly conduct, with the eighteenth-century homicide rate of Philadelphia being twice as high as London. The disparity between the classes tended to engender criminal activities on the part of the lower classes, such as thievery, murder, and prostitution.

The urban population of Philadelphia, both elite and working class, faced a disaster of major proportion when the yellow fever epidemic hit Philadelphia in 1793. That year alone, between four and five thousand persons died from the disease. The epidemics struck almost yearly for the next ten years—the worst year being 1798. The elite, to avoid infection, fled the city, leaving the working classes and the needy behind. It was not unusual for a master to inform his slaves that since they were black they would not be infected with the disease to maintain calm. Dr. Benjamin Rush, a signer of the Declaration of Independence, was a major factor in the treating of the yellow fever epidemic.

The mix of the population in the state continued to diversify as more and more immigrants arrived in Pennsylvania, predominately from Western Europe. They brought with them many of their own customs and beliefs and were drawn to Pennsylvania due to its tolerance of other religions and tenets. However, this created even more of a fractured populous as time progressed.

ARTS AND CULTURE

During this tumultuous period, Pennsylvania, and particularly Philadelphia, continued to be one of the foremost cultural centers in the colonies. Educational facilities flourished, mainly for the elite classes. In addition, in 1765, Pennsylvania established the first medical school in the colonies. Finally, the Constitution of 1790 authorized a public school system in the state.

Philadelphia was a center for intellectuals of the time, and in 1769 Benjamin Franklin was instrumental in establishing the American Philosophical Society. The Society was a major factor in establishing to the rest of the world that there were great minds among the colonies; it was viewed with great respect by its European counterparts.

The arts in Philadelphia were also flourishing. In the realm of literature, the first American novelists appeared during this early period. The two major writers were Charles Brockden Brown (1771–1810), with novels titled *Edgar Huntly* (1799), *Weiland* (1799), and *Arthur Mervyn* (1799), and Hugh Henry Breckenridge (1747–1816), who wrote a popular novel titled *Modern Chivalry* (1792). At the same time, painters associated with Philadelphia, such as Gilbert Stuart (1755–1828), Benjamin West (1738–1828), and Charles Peale (1741–1827) and his fellow family members were gaining a reputation not only in the colonies but in Europe as well.

Even the world of religion was taking on an independence from its European roots. For example, in 1785, the Episcopal Church in the United States separated from the Church of England. The Presbyterians soon followed suit, as did several other Protestant faiths. In 1789, John Carroll became the first Catholic bishop in America, and thereafter the American Catholics looked first to their bishop before the Vatican. All the religions became more responsive to their American members than to the religious leaders in Europe.

THE INDIANS

While much of the eastern part of Pennsylvania was free of Indians by the time of the Revolution, the western part of the state, now newly settled, was in a constant state of unrest between settlers and Indians. When the Revolutionary War broke out, many of the Indian tribes sided with the British, who encouraged them to raid the new settlements in the west. This continued throughout the wartime period.

With the end of the war, arguably the most respected Seneca Indian leader was a man named Cornplanter (Kaiiontwa'ko, meaning "by what one plants"). He was the son of a Dutch trader named John

Chief Cornplanter

Abeel and a Seneca woman. Cornplanter was extremely intelligent and had been brought up bilingual. While siding with the British during the war, he now knew he needed to make peace with the new government. Initially, in 1783, he signed a treaty at Ft. Stanwix in New York, which was never ratified by the Iroquois Confederacy.

Later in 1791, when the Constitutional Convention was meeting in Philadelphia, Cornplanter visited Philadelphia, where he met with George Washington to discuss Indian rights. He also discussed the confederation of the Iroquois Nation and their "constitution." George Washington was very impressed with Cornplanter and presented him with a medal. That same year, Cornplanter persuaded the Senecas to sign a treaty that ceded the "Erie Triangle" to the United States for a sum of $5,000 along with a grant of land along the Allegheny River south of New York. The land was to remain the property of the Seneca Indians until they decided to sell.

Cornplanter was in Philadelphia for an extended time in 1790, where he attended many Quaker meetings. The following year, the Quakers agreed to take his eldest son, Henry, and two other Indians into their school. This was followed in 1794 by an agreement that the Quakers would educate Cornplanter's people with the promise that they

Chief Cornplanter meets George Washington.

would not try to convert the students. While successful, the program only lasted three years.

The 1791 treaty was followed on November 11, 1794, by a treaty now known as the Pickering Treaty. The signers were Timothy Pickering, representing George Washington, and the sachems and war chiefs of the Six Nations Confederacy, including Cornplanter. The Pickering Treaty contained the following key element:

> *The United States will never claim the same, nor disturb them or either of the six nations, not their Indian friends residing thereon and unite with them, in the free use and enjoyment thereof: but said reservations shall remain theirs, until they choose to sell the same to the people of the United States who have the right to purchase.*

George Washington said of the Pickering Treaty: "Your great object seems to be the security of your remaining lands, and I have therefore, upon this point, meant to be sufficiently strong and clear. That in the future you cannot be defrauded of your lands; that you possess the right to sell and the right of refusing to sell your lands" (President George Washington to Chief Cornplanter of the Senecas). (*Note:* In 1953, the U.S. Congress passed thirteen termination laws that in effect terminated all previous treaties with the Indians.)

This period ends with a relatively quiet atmosphere both in Pennsylvania and the new nation as a whole. At this time, states such as Pennsylvania, while part of a new nation, still had strong feelings about the role of the federal government versus state government.

CHAPTER SIX

EAST MEETS WEST
(1800–1850)

GENERAL HISTORY

As the new century began, the state of Pennsylvania began to expand into what was then known as the "frontier"—and it was. The Appalachian Mountains were no longer viewed as a strong deterrent to growth. Immigrants were arriving looking for land, and most of the arable land east of the mountains was already settled—hence the push to the west. Along with this push came a realization for the state governing bodies that their responsibilities were also expanding with a new and different set of clientele, no longer driven primarily by the wants of Philadelphia.

As the period progressed, the state found itself, willingly or unwillingly, to be involved at the national level, predominately on the issues of slavery and tariffs. The period was one of considerable change within the state and an adjustment to the needs of a national government.

NATIONAL

During the period 1800–1850, Pennsylvania was a compliant contributor on the national level. In the later period, the residents of the state watched warily as the southern states began to not only dominate the Democratic Party but also much of the debate at the national level. The state was prospering, moving along a fairly steady course in their development of a state-level democracy, and life was good.

Commodore Perry at Battle of Lake Erie.

When storm clouds arose between the United States and England leading to the War of 1812, the federal government again asked the states to provide manpower for the U. S. military. Pennsylvania was asked to supply fourteen thousand men, and more than three times that amount actually volunteered. The main actions of the war in Pennsylvania were the blockade of the Delaware River and the Battle of Lake Erie.

As a result of the naval war of 1812, in 1816 Congress authorized the building of nine warships to be named *Alabama, Delaware, New Hampshire, New York, North Carolina, Ohio, Pennsylvania, Vermont,* and *Virginia.* The *Pennsylvania* was the largest sailing warship ever

USS Pennsylvania *(1846)*

built for the U.S. Navy. Its keel was laid in 1821, but construction was not completed until 1837. In 1842, it became the receiving ship for the Norfolk Navy Yard. In 1861, it was burned to the waterline to prevent the Confederacy from acquiring the ship.

In 1846, when war clouds once again appeared on the horizon, this time with Mexico, Pennsylvania responded to the call for troops. The federal government requested six regiments within thirty days. The state fielded nine complete regiments. Two of the regiments served with General Scott in Mexico, and serving with these units were Pennsylvanians who would later serve in the Civil War, including George McClellan, George Meade, Winfield Scott Hancock, Andrew Humphrey, and George McCall.

There were also some outstanding Pennsylvania natives involved in the national political scene, and the residents of the state were justly proud of them. First, Lancaster native James Buchanan began an illustrious national-level career when he was named ambassador to Russia in 1832 under Andrew Jackson. Later he became secretary of state for the James Polk administration, and later still minister to Great Britain under the Franklin Pierce administration. Second, George Mifflin Dallas served as the vice president of the United States in the Polk administration. Third, David Wilmot, a member of the U.S. Congress, proposed the Wilmot Proviso, which stated that there would be no slavery in any of the new states formed out of the territory purchased from Mexico. Pennsylvania had approved the annexation of Texas and New Mexico but did not want slavery to move west to the new states.

Pennsylvania's main interests at the national level during this period were the questions of slavery and tariffs on imported products. With its many manufacturers of products to be sold on the national level, the state maintained a requirement for high levels of tariffs on imported goods, much like the majority of the northern states.

On the individual level, the issue of the continuation of slavery became one of the focal points for the people of Pennsylvania. The Quaker influence had a major impact in the abolitionist movement that tended to be centered in Philadelphia. As early as 1829 many Quakers in Pennsylvania were for the emancipation of all Negroes on a national level. Actions of the state legislature that had national impact included an 1826 act that outlawed the kidnapping of escaped slaves in order to return them to their masters, an 1827 act that forbade the selling of slaves in the State of Pennsylvania, an 1832 act that required free Negroes to carry passes thereby barring escaping slaves from entering the state, and an 1847 act that forbade the use of Pennsylvania jails to hold fugitive slaves. The abolitionist movement grew steadily during this period. At this time, Columbia (near Lancaster) was a main transit point for the escaping slaves. Southerners searching for their escaped slaves remarked that they could trace them as far as Columbia, Pennsylvania, but there they just disappeared. They reputedly said, "There must be an underground railroad out of the place!" thus giving rise to the term "underground railroad" for escaping slaves.

Women's rights also became a Pennsylvania issue on the national level. Mrs. Lucretia Mott, a Quaker minister, was one of the four women to form the American Anti-Slavery Society in Philadelphia. This organization soon took on a national presence not only for blacks but for women. In 1848, Mrs. Mott continued her fight for equal rights by joining with Elizabeth Cady Stanton for the Seneca Falls conference on women's rights.

By the end of the period, Pennsylvania had become the second largest state, next only to New York, and its political importance in Washington did not go unnoticed.

INTERNAL

The western section of Pennsylvania started becoming a major political problem for the state in the late 1700s, and the nineteenth century brought it into clear focus. Political decisions could no longer be based solely on the desires of the eastern part of the state—the west had become a viable force in Pennsylvania politics. For example, based on the shifting demographics for the state, it had been decided that the state capital should be moved to a location more western—hence the move to Lancaster. This move did little to placate the western inhabitants of the state, so finally, in 1810, the state legislature passed an act that moved the capital to a new location—a town named Harrisburg. The move would be effective as of the year 1812.

The city of Harrisburg is named for John Harris, who operated a ferry across the Susquehanna River near the town. It was farther west than Lancaster and yet still eastern enough to allow for good commerce and communications with the major locations on the East Coast. When the discussions became known regarding the potential moving of the capital to Harrisburg, Mr. John Harris, by deed, conveyed "4 acres and 13 perches to be held in trust until the Legislature sees fit to use it." In 1810, it became a reality, and the property became the site of the new capitol, with an effective date of October of 1812.

Construction of the new building began in May of 1819, and the building was completed on January 1, 1822, at a cost of $135,000. The building, designed by a British architect named Stephen Hills, served as the state capitol building, known as the red brick capitol, until it was destroyed by a fire in 1897.

In the interim period, between 1812 and 1822, the legislature met in the Dauphin County Courthouse. This was an inconvenience to

The first capitol building in Harrisburg (1822–1897).

some, but to the western counties it was considered a victory as the capital had now been moved to a more central location for the state.

The saga of the state capital typifies the tenor of the times. The western counties were now exerting their "muscle" to become an integral part of the state, which had previously been totally controlled by Philadelphia. This struggle would continue throughout the period as Pittsburgh became a rising star and the prominence of Philadelphia began to fade. Philadelphia was no longer the center of Pennsylvania. Even a disastrous fire in Pittsburgh on April 10, 1845, that caused over $9 million worth of damage ($254 million in current value) to the city did little to lessen the growing importance of the city.

The western part of the state came into prominence during the War of 1812 with the Battle of Lake Erie. In 1813, the United States took action to have six vessels built in Erie to serve as warships on the lake. At the time, the settlement of Erie had a total of five hundred residents, so skilled workers had to be imported to build the ships. The workforce came from Pittsburgh, Philadelphia, and other locations, and many remained in Erie after the work was completed. Daniel Dobbins, a shipmaster in Erie, supervised the work along with Noah Brown from New York. The work was finished by July 1813, but the new ships were not able to go into action—the British had blockaded the harbor. On August 1, 1813, the British lifted the blockade of Erie due to a shortage of supplies, and Perry was able to take command of the new ships. At this point the British ships entered the lake to fulfill their mission of controlling Lake Erie and prevent Perry from assisting Detroit, currently under British control. On September 8, 1813, a naval battle took place on Lake Erie that resulted in the first decisive naval victory for the U.S. Navy. Detroit was saved, and the commander of the U.S. ships, Captain Oliver H. Perry, became a national hero. The location of the battle, Lake Erie, put a new focus on the western part of the state. Many of the sailors of the fleet remained in the Erie area after the cessation of hostilities.

The ordinary citizen was becoming more active in the governing of the state and not leaving politics in the hands of the wealthy class. For example, in 1808, Simon Snyder of Selinsgrove, in what today is Snyder County, was the first non-aristocrat to be elected governor of the state. He served in that capacity for nine years. And in 1817, Pennsylvania became the first state to have a nominating convention with delegates, thereby not relying on representatives from the legislature.

The western area of the state was not the only rival for attention during this period. There was a genuine struggle over education between the classes. The aristocratic class believed that only their children deserved to be educated, and that would be done by private schools. The working classes, on the other hand, pushed very hard for a public school system, and midway through this time period breakthroughs began to be made.

First, in 1830, Western University was founded in Pittsburgh. Today, the school is known as the University of Pittsburgh. At approximately the same time, the Farmer's High School was founded, which grew into the Pennsylvania State College, now the Pennsylvania State University, with an early emphasis on agriculture. The school is located in the Nittany Valley near the geographic center of the state.

Basic education for all children became a reality in 1834 when the Free School Act was passed, establishing a system of public schools in the state. The act was heavily backed by Timothy Pickering, Samuel Breck, and Thaddeus Stevens—a member of the Pennsylvania House of Representatives. The act established each county as a school division, and each ward, township, and borough in each county was to be a school district. When voted on, of the 987 districts in the state, 502 voted for the act and 274 voted against it, with the western counties being more receptive to the law. Once the act was passed, constant quarreling broke out, until finally, with the support of Thaddeus Stevens, a new act was passed in August 1845, with only minor changes. By 1840, there were three thousand public schools in the state, and by 1850 that number had grown to ten thousand. These schools served mainly the working classes, as the aristocrats continued to use private schools to educate their children.

Along with geographic and cultural differences, there was another undercurrent present in the state in the 1830s—that of the anti-Freemason movement. Freemasonry was looked upon with mistrust, as it was seen as a secret organization imbedded in a free society—one that required an oath of allegiance to the organization and not the country. The Freemason movement was national in nature and was generally made up of well-connected aristocrats, manifesting itself strongly in Pennsylvania where it was highly suspected of initiating political decisions behind closed doors. Thaddeus Stevens was elected to the Pennsylvania House of Representatives in 1833 as an anti-Mason, and in the state elections of 1834 and 1838 Governor Joseph Ritner was elected and then reelected governor on an anti-Mason ticket. For the anti-Masonic element, his election represented their highest-level elected officer yet. In 1838, he ran for reelection against David R. Porter, a Democrat. Ritner lost the election by about five thousand votes and demanded a recount, claiming voter fraud against him and the other anti-Mason candidates running for the state legislature. Governor Ritner lost his claim of victory and bowed to defeat; however, the candidates for the state legislature were not so compliant. The focus of the voter fraud centered on the Northern Liberties area of Philadelphia, where about five thousand votes were in question. A panel of Democratic return judges threw out the entire five thousand votes and certified the Democratic candidates as elected. At the same time, the Whig judges declared their candidates the victors and issued them certificates of election. Both parties sent their certificates to the state capital for certification. The Whig state party immediately certified their candidates as valid.

The legislature met on December 4, 1838, in a state of confusion. On the House side of the legislature two separate sets of representatives were in the room—the Whigs and the Democrats. William Hopkins headed the Democrat contingent, and Thomas Cunningham the Whig delegation. Both declared their party candidates to be the victors, and tensions rose. Demonstrators from Philadelphia soon appeared, and the tensions rose to a level of potential rioting among the demonstrators.

Outgoing Governor Ritner, declaring the capital to be in the hands of the riotous mob, called up the commandant of the militia to assist in maintaining calm in Harrisburg, but the commandant at Carlisle Barracks, Captain Sumner, refused. The governor then called upon President Van Buren for troops to protect the state from domestic violence. President Van Buren also refused, stating that the riots arose not from opposition to the laws but from a political contest.

Finally, about a thousand militia members arrived in Harrisburg and assisted in quelling the riots. On December 23, the Senate recognized the Democratic element led by William Hopkins as the legitimate delegation, and the domestic violence ceased. The event has become known as the Buckshot War, as attributed to a Whig member who threatened that the mob "should feel ball and buckshot before the day was over."

The year 1838 also saw the adoption of a new constitution for Pennsylvania. A constitutional convention called in 1837 had drafted a new constitution, which became effective in 1838. The new constitution contained the following changes:

- It reduced the governor's power of appointment, thereby increasing the number of elected positions in the state.
- It shortened the terms of office for many of the appointments.
- It disenfranchised the free Negro vote but did not provide voting rights to females.

In general, the new constitution put more power in the hands of the electorate and provided them protection from abuses of power by those in governmental positions.

But the internal political scene continued to ferment with political activity complicated by two factors: first, the large increase of European immigrants entering the state, and second, the continual "Negro problem." As early as 1829, supporters of emancipation, such as Mrs. Fanny Wright Darusmont, began giving public speeches about emancipation and abolition. Then, in May 1838, Pennsylvania Hall, built by the abolitionists, was burned just three days after its dedication. Firefighters sprayed only the surrounding buildings and ignored the newly built hall.

While having to deal with the "Negro problem" and increasing immigration, the "Indian problem" in Pennsylvania by the end of this period had been "solved" as the local Indians, including the Susquehannock, the Delaware, the Eire, and the Lenape tribes, had all been relocated to the Oklahoma territory.

Later, in May 1844, the Native American Party, also known as the American Republican Party, was formed. The party was particularly active in the Kensington area of Philadelphia, heavily populated by Irish immigrants. The party platform extended the period of naturalization to twenty-one years, only native-born could be elected to office, and foreign interference in all institutions, social, religious, and political was rejected. The platform was directed mainly at the Roman Catholic Church and immigrants in general.

On May 3, 1844, party members went to the Kensington area, set up a platform, and proceeded to espouse their beliefs. They returned again on May 6, and this time a riot broke out, as Nativist party members proceeded to loot and burn both St. Micale's Church and St. Charles Seminary. The Nativists then returned to Philadelphia, where they burned St. Augustine's Catholic Church. At this point, martial law was enforced for one week in hopes that the situation would calm down. All of the rioters arrested were tried. The non-Irish detainees were tried by non-Catholic juries, who found all of the Nativists not guilty. However, all of the Irish detainees, tried by the same juries, were found guilty. The Nativist movement later became known as the "Know-Nothing Society," and subsequently in 1853 the "Know-Nothing Party," and it remained active to late in the century.

Women also were active in efforts to receive equal rights in the state during this period. In 1847, Jane Grey Swisshelm, an abolitionist and women's rights advocate, founded a newspaper, the *Pittsburgh Saturday Visitor*, and used this newspaper to impart her views to the populous. Her essays regarding a woman's right to own property led the state legislature, in 1848, to enact a bill allowing women the right to own property.

Changes of the political atmosphere for the state were occurring rapidly during this period. The common man was wresting political power away from the aristocratic elements, and a major shift was occurring geographically—the focus of the state was shifting from Philadelphia to be more inclusive of the western part of the state.

The internal competitions between the various groups were very far afield from the tolerance envisaged by the founder, William Penn.

INDUSTRY

The industrial age burst upon the scene in Pennsylvania during this period. The state had always had a mixture of craftsmen and small-business enterprises, but with the turn of the century, the entire picture of the industrial age came into focus. One of the reasons for this change was Benjamin Franklin, who upon his return from Europe had established in 1788 an organization known as the Pennsylvania Society for the Encouragement of Manufactures and Useful Arts. This society encouraged artisans and manufacturers from Europe to come to the United States and establish their businesses. In 1788, the Society sponsored a contest to improve the textile manufacturing in the state. The main areas involved in this massive change were agriculture, the coal industry, textiles, manufacturing, and transportation systems including canals, railroads, paved roads, and bridges, which were needed to transport goods. For the sake of clarity, each of these areas will be treated separately.

Inventions

One invention that had an impact on the industry of the day was the invention of a land-based self-propelled vehicle that later became known as the automobile. It made its first U.S. appearance in 1804 in Philadelphia. That year, Oliver Evans is credited with developing a steam-driven dredge to use on a local river. He then placed wheels on the equipment, enabling it to use steam power to move without assistance along the river banks. While not officially an automobile, it was the first use of steam power coupled with wheels that could move a piece of equipment along the ground unassisted.

Agriculture

While agriculture had always been a major part of the Pennsylvania economy, it was predominately a manual-labor industry. That changed starting around 1820, when Joseph and Robert Smith of Berks County designed a practical cast iron plow. They also created a thresher that in one single operation could both clean and thresh grain. Both pieces of equipment were quickly adopted by the farmers. By 1850, mechanical farm equipment such as steam tractors and mowers were in general use throughout the state.

Coal

While coal had been employed for heating in Europe for many years, the early settlers in America were dependent on wood, which was plentiful, for heating in lieu of imported coal from Europe. However, as American cities developed interest in coal as a fuel, its use increased.

Coal mining has long been synonymous with Pennsylvania. The first reference to the presence of coal was in 1751 when bituminous coal was discovered along the Kiskiminetas River near Saltsburg. Early uses of coal followed and in 1797, the Penn family began selling the rights to mine coal in the Pittsburgh area. In 1803, the first shipment of bituminous coal left Pittsburgh. It consisted of 350 tons shipped on the steamer the *Louisiana* on the Mississippi River. That shipment eventually made its way to Philadelphia, where it was sold for 37.5 cents a bushel. A year later, William Boyd shipped an ark (boatload) of coal from Clearfield to Columbia in Lancaster County via the Susquehanna River. Shipments in the east also were made in 1807, 1813, and 1814.

While the presence of anthracite coal was known in the mid-1700s, it was not until the early 1800s that its use for general heating purposes was realized. One of the pioneers in this area was Judge Jesse Fell, who recorded in his diary on February 11, 1807, that he had successfully experimented with the use of anthracite coal in a grate for heating purposes. Quickly adopted for local use, the general use of anthracite coal took several years to gain general acceptance. With this acceptance, the coal mining industry flourished.

One of the early pioneer companies in the coal mining industry was the Lehigh Coal and Navigation Company, which was formed in 1820. By 1824, the company was in full operation and that year managed to ship nine thousand tons to the marketplace. Interest continued to grow. In 1827, the company mine at Summit Hill constructed a gravity railroad eighteen miles long from the mine to Mauch Chunk, a port on the Lehigh canal (now known as Jim Thorpe). It was the first railroad line in the state over one mile long. All grades from the various mines in the area ran downhill to the port for further shipment to the cities. The cars were loaded with coal and simply rolled down the tracks. Initially, to return the empty cars to the mines, donkeys rode down in the cars and pulled the empty cars back to the mines. Then in 1845, a cable from Mauch Chunk to the top of the mountain was initiated to return the empty cars. This gravity fed railroad line was 18 miles long and was the first railroad line in the state over one mile in length. The technology used for the railroad later became the technology employed for the early roller coasters in amusement parks.

Later, in the mid 1830s, the coal industry devised a new system to deliver coal across the mountains. The coal would be loaded onto

Gravity railroad at Mauch Chunk.

Packet boat aboard a railroad car.

packet boats employed on the canal systems. When the boats reached the mountainous area where canals were not possible, they were placed on railroad flatbeds. The railroad cars could then be taken up the mountain and down the other side, where once again the boats could be placed in a canal.

As the coal industry progressed, so did other industries. One of the first industries to feel the impact of the increased availability of coal was the iron industry. In 1818, Colonel Isaac Meason, owner of the Plumsock Iron Works, began using what came to be known as coke (produced by heating coal at extreme temperatures) in lieu of coal for iron production. It had been discovered that coke produced a more stable and pure heat. This ironworks was the first iron rolling mill west of the Alleghenies. Then, in 1833, the first beehive ovens capable of producing coke in large quantities in the United States began operation near Connellsville. The ovens were named "beehive" because they were made of brick and formed in the shape of a beehive. The oven's function was used to convert coal to coke. That same year, Dr. Frederick W. Geisenheimer secured a patent for smelting pig iron with anthracite and in 1836 built the Lucy furnace near Pottsville, where the new process was initiated. The technique of using anthracite for smelting became known as the "blast furnace" technique, and this technique became the norm for the iron/steel industry.

As the coal industry continued to grow, it had multiple impacts on other industries, such as the iron smelting business, and transportation systems such as railroad and canals. It also had a major impact on the domestic scene, with more efficient heating of homes and a decreased demand for wood-burning stoves. With this in mind, the state of Pennsylvania, in 1836, established the Pennsylvania Geologic Survey to map and record the state's natural resources.

Many immigrants looked at the mines as a way to immediately earn money upon entering the country, as coal mining was a major employer always looking for more miners. Language was not a barrier for employment, but the work was hard and the conditions intolerable, to the extent that in 1842 the first strike affecting over two hundred miners was called over working conditions. The miners working in the Minersville area of Schuylkill County marched to Pottsville to protest against the low wages. The protest was broken up by the local militia. Later, in 1848, John Bates organized five thousand miners in what became known as "Bates' Union," again in protest of low wages. The union collapsed in 1849, but the stage was set for a long continuation of conflict between the miners and the managers of the mines.

Iron Production

The production of iron using furnaces had been an industry in the colonies since the earliest days, and by the time of the 1800s there were over five hundred iron ore furnaces in the state of Pennsylvania.

Iron ore furnace, Caledonia

These furnaces were initially fired using wood or charcoal and later bituminous coal or coke. However, the industry changed greatly with the introduction of anthracite coal to fire the furnaces in 1840. Anthracite, unlike bituminous coal, provided a higher and sustainable heat source for the smelting process. With this change the iron industry in Pennsylvania flourished.

The increased capability for iron production was well received by other industries. The steam engine required rolled iron for the manufacturing of boilers, and the birth of the railroad in the United States created a heavy demand for iron railroad tracks. In addition, there was still the need for iron in the manufacturing of tools, stoves, kettles, and cannonballs. Pennsylvania became the major producer of iron for the United States.

While iron production increased during this period, Europe remained the source for much of the world's steel. All steel employed in the United States at this time was imported from Europe, specifically the United Kingdom. But that would soon change. New steel-production technology would soon come to Pennsylvania, making Pittsburgh an industrial giant. Steel production began in Pittsburgh in 1866.

Textiles

The manufacturing of textiles became a significant industry in Pennsylvania for two reasons: the German Palatines brought their weaving skills with them (especially useful for hosiery production) and the easy availability of water to power the mills. Prior to 1825, over two-thirds of the textile production was done in the home, but that year Thomas Fisher convinced the domestic weavers to locate their machines in one building where weavers worked independently but the products were sold by one agent. The industry flourished because of this consolidation. By 1840, the home industry had been replaced by the mills.

Northern Liberties, an area adjacent to Philadelphia, and specifically the town of Manayunk, became a major textile manufacturing area. Initially, the mills would just produce the yarn and that would be given to the over five thousand weavers in Philadelphia to produce the finished product. Over time the mills not only produced the yarn but also employed the weavers to create the textiles. Weaving was no longer a major cottage industry.

Along with woolen products, mills also produced items made of silk. Silk had been produced in the state as early as 1750, but by 1839, silk farming was abandoned and only the production of silk products continued. Power looms were introduced in 1837 to increase the production of such products as ribbons, fringes, and tassels. The textile industry in Pennsylvania not only made products to wear, such as hosiery and apparel, but it also became a leading manufacturer of carpets.

As the textile industry flourished, so did the need for labor, and the mills turned to children to fill the gap. The 1820 census for the city of Philadelphia found that 40 percent of the 1,100 workers employed by a total of thirty-nine textile mills were children, some as young as eight years old. Finally, in 1837, the issue of child labor was addressed by the Pennsylvania General Assembly. Hearings were held and testimonies were gathered, but it was not until 1849 that legislative action was taken:

- ◆ Children were restricted to working only ten hours a day and sixty hours per week.
- ◆ Children under the age of twelve were prohibited from working in the textile factories.
- ◆ Children under sixteen were permitted to work provided they attended school for three months a year.

These initial laws were never tightly enforced—the textile mills continued to employ children, and families in need of money continued to misrepresent the ages of their youngsters in order to have them work in the mills. By 1850, there were 105 cotton mills, 40 dye and print facilities, and over 5,500 people employed in the textile industry in the state.

Canals

The creation of canals for use in transporting goods had long been a dream for Pennsylvania. As early as 1690, William Penn thought of a canal to connect the Delaware River with the Susquehanna River; however, nothing developed until 1797. By this time, the demand for lumber and other products from the interior had, along with the population, increased greatly. Another factor was the more general use of coal for heating, which made it essential that more efficient transportation from points of internal origin to populated areas be developed. Subsequently, the first canal, the Conewago, was built in 1797. This canal was constructed on the west bank of the Susquehanna River near York Haven to provide passage for boats around the Conewago Falls, thereby connecting river traffic with Columbia, which was connected to Philadelphia by the Pennsylvania Turnpike.

This early canal was the only canal in Pennsylvania until 1828. Progress was slow in coming, and citizens in the early 1800s began to press for a public works program that would provide a means of transporting needed items such as lumber, coal, and manufactured goods from all areas of the state, including the area west of the Allegheny Mountains. Finally, in 1824, the state assembly passed an authorization for a state public works project regarding canals. The following year, the assembly established a Board of Canal Commissioners, and the next year, 1826, they enacted a program for public canal and railroad works. This action is largely responsible for revolutionizing the transportation and industrial profile of the state. The act remained in effect until 1857, at a cost of over $33 million.

The first canal created through the act was constructed by the Union Canal Company in 1828, which succeeded in joining the Schuylkill with the Susquehanna and thereby provided a connection between Middletown and Philadelphia. The success of this endeavor led to a major increase in the construction of canals within the state.

The year 1834 was a benchmark for the building of canals, when the Pennsylvania Canal was completed. This canal connected the western part of the state with the east and surmounted the Allegheny Mountains by employing a portage railroad to carry the canal boats across the mountains. The Allegheny Railroad ran between Hollidaysburg and Johnstown. It carried canal boats, passengers, and cargo by rail across the mountains. Canals boats were actually taken out of the water, put on rail cars, and then taken over the mountains.

Initially, horses or mules were used on the portage railroad. Later a cable system was installed. The thirty-six-mile Allegheny Portage Railroad consisted of eighteen lift-locks between Columbia and Hollidaysburg and sixty-six between Johnstown and Pittsburgh. The canal actually crossed both the Allegheny and the Susquehanna rivers by bridges. These two rivers run in a southerly direction, while the canals were east to west in their direction.

The building of canals spread across the state, and by the year of 1840, canal mileage totaled 726 miles with another 208 miles under construction. Some important accomplishments were connecting the Susquehanna Valley with Baltimore in 1840 and the inclusion of Lake Erie into the canal system. But the heyday was short-lived. By the 1850s, the competition from the railroads proved too strong for the canals, and as early as 1843 the state began disposing of its canals to private companies.

The use of canals ended first in the western part of the state, quickly supplanted by railroads. The use of canals as envisaged by both George Washington and William Penn had seen its day, although it did not completely cease operation in Pennsylvania until the Lehigh Coal and Navigation Company shut down its canals in 1931.

Railroads

Canals and railroads in Pennsylvania had a very early connection. The first railroad in Pennsylvania is recorded in 1809–1810. It consisted of wagons on rails, drawn by horses or mules, connecting the quarry at Avondale with a boat landing on Ridley Creek. Other early "railroads" appeared in these days—all pulled by horse or mule. The Mauck Chunk Railroad, built in 1827 on a gravity-fed basis, was built to move coal from the mines to the river for further transportation to the cities—it was not a true railroad, although it did create interest in further development (see page 81).

In 1823, the Delaware & Hudson Canal Company was created to carry coal from the fields near Carbondale, Pennsylvania, to New York via a canal system. By 1825, they began to plan for a railroad system to augment the canals, and in 1828, the company contracted with two

Stourbridge Lion

The Stourbridge Lion—*the first locomotive to run on rails in America, now in the Smithsonian Institution in Washington, D.C.*
SMITHSONIAN INSTITUTION.

English firms—Foster, Rastrick, and Company and the Steven firm—to build locomotives for their use. Four engines were built, the first of which, the *Stourbridge Lion*, arrived in the United States that same year. It was assembled at the West Point Foundry in New York and was first tested under steam in 1829. That same year it made its first run on August 8 in Honesdale, Pennsylvania, thus marking the first occurrence of rail use in the United States. By 1834, the *Stourbridge Lion* was no longer in use—it proved to be too heavy. By 1830, U.S. manufacturers were making locomotives better suited to the tracks in the United States.

During this same period a major transportation problem was solved using a combination of canals and railroads. The Allegheny mountain range runs north and south across the state, making early transportation between the eastern and western parts extremely difficult. The Allegheny Portage Railroad solved the problem in 1833. The solution consisted of a thirty-six-mile route over the mountains and combined various forms of transportation. The first railroad tunnel in the United States was built in 1833 east of Johnstown to accommodate the Allegheny Portage. At the Hollidaysburg end, the arriving boats were placed on railroad cars that were then moved up the inclines (called planes) by stationary engines. Initially, the rail cars were pulled by horse power at the flat terrain areas and were later replaced with steam engines. This ingenious system connected the western canal system with the east, and in 1840 a passenger could make the trip from Philadelphia to Pittsburgh in four days instead of twenty-three by coach.

Another innovation to conquer the mountainous terrain of the state for the railroads occurred in 1833 when the first railroad tunnel in the United States was dug four miles east of Johnstown, Pennsylvania. It was part of the Pennsylvania Portage Railroad.

One of the early U.S. manufacturers of steam engines was the predecessor of the Baldwin Locomotive Works in Philadelphia. On November 23, 1832, their first steam engine, known as *Old Ironsides*, made its first test run on the Philadelphia, Germantown & Norristown Railroad which at that time pulled the cars by horsepower. Just two years earlier, the entire United States had only twenty-three miles of railroad track for steam engines. In 1835, the Philadelphia, Germantown & Norristown Railroad became the first railroad in the state to be powered by steam engines. It served the Philadelphia area and was the forerunner of the development of the railroad in Pennsylvania. By 1836, there was a total of 314 miles of railroad in the state, which represented a quarter of all the railroad tracks in the entire United States.

Other early railroads developed at this time were Philadelphia & Reading Railroad (1833), Pennsylvania Railroad (1840), and the Lehigh Valley Railroad (1846).

Old Ironsides

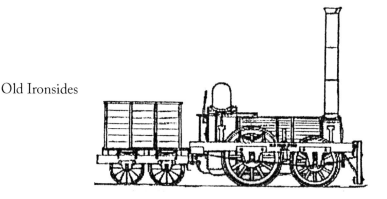

By 1850, there was 822.47 miles of railroad track in the state of Pennsylvania, which represented approximately 9 percent of the total track mileage in the United States. The tracks were utilized for the movement of such commodities as coal.

Miscellaneous Industries

Several smaller industries were also a part of the industrial scene of Pennsylvania in this period.

Carpets and rugs: Pennsylvania, specifically Philadelphia, led the United States in the production of carpets and rugs until 1890, when New York and New England became the new centers for carpet manufacturing.

Beer: Breweries became prevalent in the early 1800s. The most famous is the Yuengling Brewery of Pottsville, founded in 1829. It holds the distinction of being the oldest continually operated brewery in the United States.

Cigars: By 1840, cigar factories in Pennsylvania were producing 33 million cigars a year as well as the boxes to keep them in.

Steamboats: By 1809, steam ferries were regularly running between Philadelphia and Camden, New Jersey, to be followed in 1818 by regular steamboat runs from Philadelphia to New York and Baltimore. In the west, steamboats also became an essential part of transportation as steamboats were used from Pittsburgh down the Ohio River to New Orleans. Steamboat activity in the state peaked between 1850 and 1860 and decreased thereafter as railroads became the dominant mode of transportation.

People

When the colonial period ended, only about one-fourth of the state—largely the eastern part—was actually populated. The 1790 census counted 434,373 persons in the state. By comparison, the 1840 census lists the state population as 1,735,033.

The majority of the immigrants to the state during this period were from England and Ireland. Later, in 1840, German and Irish immigration increased considerably while immigrants from Scotland declined. Immigrants tended to settle in areas where their fellow countrymen lived, which led to a patchwork-quilt effect developing in the state. The English settled in the eastern part of the state, the Germans just west of this area, and the Scotch and Irish in the central, southwest, and northwest areas. Most of the new immigrants went to work in the factories, while the "native born" represented the largest portion of the agricultural workforce. Quaker influence continued to wane during the period as various other religions became more firmly established.

At the beginning of the 1800s, about 90 percent of the population either worked in agriculture or in small family industries. The workforce distribution changed greatly during the course of the next fifty years. As the population grew an average of 30 percent a decade, the demand for unskilled laborers increased. Many of the new immigrants either went into the mines or other industrial enterprises where no previous skill training was necessary.

The 1850 census for Philadelphia County shows the following ethnic groups of new immigrants: African: 19,301; English: 17,500; German: 22,700; Irish: 72,312; Jewish: 3,000. This brought the total Philadelphia County population to 408,761.

The native-born Americans began to resent the fact that the various ethnic groups tended to form their own ethnic areas within the towns and did not assimilate rapidly into the local society, maintaining their native language, customs, religions, and dietary requirements.

As the population grew, so did the cities that received the new immigrants. The following shows the growth of the major cities between 1800 and 1850:

City	1800 Population	1850 Population
Philadelphia	41,226	121,376
Pittsburgh	1,565	46,601
Harrisburg		7,834
Erie	81	5,850

These statistics show the movement of the settlers from the Eastern Seaboard to what was then called the Western Frontier.

In addition, the religious complexion of the state was changing as well. The most prevalent religion was Presbyterian, with 15.57 percent of the population, followed by Methodist at 14.77 percent, Lutheran at 11.31 percent, and Roman Catholic at 3.6 percent. The Quaker population had slipped to only 2.65 percent of the state's population.

Pennsylvanians were generally sympathetic to the abolitionist cause, but there were enough anti-abolitionists in Pennsylvania that racial tensions and frequent riots occurred. In 1837, the Pennsylvania Anti-Slavery Society was formed in Philadelphia to be followed the next year by the formation of a Pennsylvania chapter of the national organization—the Anti-Slavery Society.

The African American population tended to center in Philadelphia, where they soon settled in the western area of Philadelphia, known as "Black Bottom," and where black businesses arose between 1820 and 1870. Since blacks were forbidden from learning new skills they utilized the skills they knew—many of which the general population did not want to do.

Examples of the black business initiatives include a trade guild for caterers and masters formed in 1820 that supplied domestic help to the wealthy residents of the town and provided what became a lucrative business of catering. African American men, such as Bogle, Augustin, Prossey, Dorsey, Jones, and Mintouany, prospered in this business venture. One man, James Forten, used his skills to establish a sail-making business that eventually earned him an estate over $100,000.

Arts and Culture

Throughout the period, Philadelphia continued to be one of the main cultural centers of the nation. The capital city maintained a leading position in the publication of magazines and periodicals such as the *Farm Journal*, founded in 1827, which is still in publication today. During the 1830s, Philadelphia had more newspapers published on a daily basis than any other city in the country.

The arts flourished as well. Artists such as Edward Hicks, Charles Rembrandt Peale, and John Lewis were all active and sought after for commissions. In addition, in the 1830s, Philadelphia became the theatrical center of the nation for both drama and music, leading in 1845 to the premiere of the first American opera—a work by William Henry Fry titled *Lenora.*

Societies for the advancement of science and the arts also sprang up—mostly in Philadelphia. Some of these included the Philadelphia Association of Fine Arts (1805), the Academy of Natural Science (1812), the Franklin Institute (1824), and the American Association of Geologists (1840). While these organizations were based in Philadelphia, their impact was felt on a national as well as international level.

THE INDIANS

In the early part of the post-Revolutionary period, Chief Cornplanter's association with the Quakers continued to flourish even though some of his fellow leaders were strongly opposed to any assimilation with whites. Cornplanter's close relationship with the non-native Pennsylvanians persisted until after the War of 1812, when he became disillusioned with the treatment of his fellow Indians. In a reversal of his policy, Cornplanter closed all his schools, dismissing the missionaries. Cornplanter never completely severed his ties with the Quakers for the remainder of his life. He died on February 18, 1836, in his home on the Cornplanter tract. His descendents continued to live on the tract but in lesser and lesser numbers until 1965, when the tract was flooded for the Kinzua Dam.

By 1850, the Indians had been all but removed from Pennsylvania. The last remaining group had been relocated to the northern quadrant of the state near the New York border (the Cornplanter tract). Many of these Indians later became part of the forced relocation to Oklahoma.

By the last half of the nineteenth century, Pennsylvania's population began to move westward in search of a new industrial base. As more and more of the state's abundant natural resources were discovered, Pennsylvania began to shift from a predominantly agricultural economy to an industrial one.

The period closes with a new awareness in the state of the western movement of not only population but also the industrial base—Philadelphia was learning that it had to share its prominence with a new city: Pittsburgh. As the country grew and demands rose for natural resources, Pennsylvania became not only a center for agriculture but also a source of vital natural resources such as iron and coal. The changes in the economic base of the state also brought with them changes in the population. More and more laborers were needed for the industrial complex, thus attracting a large increase in immigrants to the state. By the end of the period, Pennsylvania, known as a major agricultural center, was emerging as a major source of natural resources with a growing industrial base.

Chapter Seven

Conflicts and Progress
(1850–1900)

General History

The period from 1850 to 1900 was one of conflict at both the national and state level. Military wars were one reason for this conflicted atmosphere, with both the bloody American Civil War and the Spanish-American War putting the United States on the world stage for the first time. In addition, there was continual conflict between labor and the new generation of management. This period saw many labor strikes—some which proved deadly—the growth of labor unions in conflict with management, and such moral issues as child labor, at both the national and state level.

Nationally, tensions arose between the Northern states and the Southern states over the issue of tariffs. The Northern states, with predominantly manufacturing economies, wanted high tariffs to protect their products from competition from European manufacturers, while the Southern states, which were mainly agricultural and imported a vast majority of their manufactured goods, wanted lower tariffs to keep their costs lower. This conflict raged on throughout the early part of this period. When they were combined with two older, highly volatile issues—the right for individual states to secede from the Union and slavery—the stage was set for an explosion.

National

At the national level, two issues were predominant during this period: slavery and tariffs. Prominent Pennsylvania politicians such as Simon

Cameron, David Wilmot, and James Buchanan struggled with these issues as they affected their state. Both Cameron and Wilmot were instrumental in forming the Republican Party and helping elect President Lincoln. David Wilmot, earlier in 1846, had written the Wilmot Proviso proposing to exclude slaves from the territory acquired from Mexico. James Buchanan, who served in the House of Representatives and the Senate and as ambassador to Russia, ran twice for the presidency. He first ran in 1853 and was defeated by Franklin Pierce. He ran for a second time in 1856 and was elected on the Democratic ticket.

Pennsylvanians were not unified in their thinking regarding slavery. Many felt that if the slaves were freed, working-class laborers would lose their jobs to African Americans, who would work for less. However, most Pennsylvanians felt that individual states did not have the right to secede from the Union.

When the Civil War actually broke out, Pennsylvania was quick to respond. The first units to be mustered were the Ringgold Light Artillery of Reading, the Logan Guards of Lewistown, the Allen Rifles of Allentown, and the Washington Artillery and the National Light Infantry, both of Pottsville. These five units, consisting of a total of 530 men, were sent immediately to Washington. Their quick arrival in Washington, on April 18, 1861, led to the units being nicknamed the "First Defenders of Washington."

In all, over 300,000 men served in the Union army from Pennsylvania and over 14,000 served in the Union navy. In contrast, over 2,000 Pennsylvania natives joined the Confederate army. African American men from Pennsylvania, once permitted, also joined the Union army. In total, 8,612 Pennsylvania African Americans enlisted. This number represents the most African American troops in the Union army for any state in the Union. When President Lincoln asked the state of Pennsylvania for fourteen regiments, he got twenty-five. Among the more notable generals from Pennsylvania were George McClellan, George Meade, Joshua Reynolds, John Geary, Winfield Hancock, David Birney, Henry Pleasanton, and John Hartranft. In addition, Governor Curtin was a staunch supporter of the Union during the entire war.

However, there was opposition to the draft. Many of the working class did not favor freeing the slaves, as they feared a new competitive working class would develop and take their jobs for lower pay. As an example, in Venango County, out of 700 drafted, 90 paid the commutation fee, 30 furnished substitutes, 140 failed to report, and practically all the rest were exempted for medical reasons.

The U.S. Navy greatly enlarged its fleet during the Civil War, and once again Pennsylvania was selected as the name for a new screw steamer. The keel was laid in 1863 and was to be named *Keywaden*, later renamed the *Pennsylvania*. The ship was never completed, and finally in 1884, it was broken up. In addition, a wooden side-wheeler steamer named *Keystone State* chartered to the U.S. Navy served the Union along the Atlantic Coast throughout the war years.

In addition to manpower, Pennsylvania was a principle supplier of food and other staples for the troops and a major arms manufacturer. The proximity of the state to the eastern battlefields proved to be a major asset in supplying the Union armies in the area.

After the Civil War, the state was split on how to handle the former Confederate states. The Democrats wanted quick restoration of the Southern states without undue political burden but to include the abolition of slavery. The Republicans wanted some kind of reform of the Southern institutions. During the Reconstruction period, two Pennsylvania members of Congress were influential in the decisions made in the legislature. William Kelly, who believed in high tariffs, which were good for Pennsylvania, acquired the name of "Pig Iron Kelly" for his insistence on the issue. He was also a strong believer in rights for African Americans. The other, Thaddeus Stevens, wanted a military occupation of the South, disempowering of the planter elite, and also wanted a redistribution of the land to provide forty-acre grants to freed slaves. He was not successful in his endeavors.

The economic panic of 1857 that followed the Mexican-American War was repeated in 1867, when an economic slowdown hit Pennsylvania and the rest of the nation. Seven years later, the failure of Jay Cooke's brokerage led to a series of depressions nationwide. The 1873 financial crisis hit the states of Pennsylvania, Virginia, and New York especially hard, with many small businesses being forced to close their doors. The crisis was particularly hard on the Pennsylvania farmers, as agricultural prices fell and many lost their farms. The 1873 depression, which lasted until 1877, was followed by economic depressions in 1884, 1886, and from 1893 to 1897. All affected both the manufacturing and agricultural bases of Pennsylvania.

Pennsylvania figured predominately in the one hundredth anniversary of the signing of the Declaration of Independence. After years of planning, on July 4, 1876, a huge Centennial Exposition was opened in the Fairmont Park area of Philadelphia by President Grant. The exposition was called the International Exhibition of Arts, Manufacturers and Products of the Soil & Mine. The main exhibition hall, known as Machinery Hall, was 1,880 feet long and covered twenty acres. It was the largest building in the world at that time. One of the buildings, the Memorial Hall, remains in use in Philadelphia today. The torch of the Statue of Liberty was on display at the exposition prior to its installation on the statue in New York Harbor.

The exposition was such a success that for the two hundredth anniversary of the signing of the Declaration of Independence in 1976, the Smithsonian Institute in Washington, D.C., installed a special exhibition in the Arts and Industries Building titled "1876: A Centennial Exhibition." The exhibition duplicated many of the machinery

Machinery Hall

Memorial Hall

Statue of Liberty torch

displays originally shown in Machinery Hall. The exhibit, intended as a temporary exhibit, was so popular that it remained on display for more than twenty years.

After the euphoria of the one hundredth anniversary, the entire nation looked inward to respond to the various economic downturns taking place. However, relations with Spain over the question of the independence of Cuba and the Philippines continued to deteriorate. Finally, after the sinking of the U.S. battleship *Maine* in Havana Harbor on February 15, 1898, President McKinley declared war on Spain in April of 1898.

The initial troop call for the state of Pennsylvania was 10,600, which was quickly filled, as was a second call for 6,370 additional troops. None of the Pennsylvania troops saw action in Cuba. However, the Fourth and Sixteenth Pennsylvania regiments did serve in Puerto Rico, and the Eleventh Regiment saw duty in the Philippines. The Eleventh Regiment was the first U.S. Army unit to engage in land combat in the Philippine Islands.

With the emergence of the United States onto the world stage the emphasis of the individual states also changed. The government and the people of Pennsylvania now had to be prepared to not only support their state government but also to have a voice in the involvement of the federal government on the international level. This transition was not an easy one for all of the citizens to make.

Internal

The internal atmosphere of the state of Pennsylvania closely resembled that of the national climate throughout the 1800s. Conflict and change were constantly occurring. The longstanding competition between the eastern and western parts of the state gained momentum as the west became a strong industrial center and in many ways overshadowed the east. Philadelphia, while maintaining its cultural advantage, was rapidly losing its industrial prowess to Pittsburgh in the west. While the competition was real, there was no move to separate the west from the east in a new state.

Early in the period, the political scene was dominated by the Democrats and the Whigs, but that was soon to change. Between 1852 and 1854, confusion reigned. The Democrats were demoralized due to the defeat of the Missouri Compromise in 1854, and the Whig party was rapidly losing ground—many were looking for a new party to align themselves with. That party became the Know-Nothing Party, which supplanted the earlier Native American Party. The Know-Nothings' rise to prominence was short-lived, however—ending after the elections of 1854. A new party on the horizon, the Republican Party, by 1860 had absorbed most of the Whigs and many of the Know-Nothings into their party. The first elected Republican governor of Pennsylvania was Andrew Curtin, but only for his second term, having initially been elected from the People's Party.

When Simon Cameron was elected to the U.S. Senate in 1866 from Pennsylvania, he founded a political dynasty that lasted well into the twentieth century: he was followed in the U.S. Senate by his son Donald Cameron and later by Mathew S. Quay and Boies Penrose. Their control of the state's Republican Party spawned a period of corruption and unscrupulous politics that lasted beyond the turn of the century.

Even with all the conflicts on the state political scene, important advances were made by the state legislature. In 1874, a new constitution was approved for the state. The important changes in the new document included the following:

- A provision was added for popular election of judges, state treasurer, and auditor general.
- The position of lieutenant governor and the Department of Internal Affairs were established.
- The Department of Public Instruction for the head of schools was established.
- The governor's term was extended from three to four years, but he could not succeed himself.
- The House of Representatives was increased to two hundred members and the Senate to fifty in the belief that larger bodies would diminish the strength of interest groups.

- The 1863 provision denying African Americans the right to vote was removed (already illegal by the Fifteenth Amendment to the U.S. Constitution).

The new state constitution was passed by over 70 percent of the population.

Other important legislation enacted during the period indicates the state's awareness of the value of education and the right of privacy when voting. In the first case, in 1887, Governor James A. Beaver appointed an industrial education commission of five members to look at the desirability of promoting technical and industrial education in the state. This led to the establishment of manual training schools in many of the cities and towns in the state. In the second case, in 1893, the legislature enacted a bill establishing the Australian ballot system in the state. This system provided for secrecy in voting and ensured voters freedom from intimidation in the voting process.

The fire destroying the capitol building in Harrisburg, 1897.

As the government grew, new state agencies were established to meet all the citizens' needs. Some established during this period include the following:

- Board of Public Charities (1869)
- Insurance Department (1873)
- Committee on Lunacy (1883) (To handle the mentally ill)
- Factory Inspectorship (1889)
- State Department of Agriculture (1895)

The legislative process met with a disaster on February 2, 1897, when the state capitol building burned to the ground. As an interim measure, a new building was built in 1899 (known as the Cobb Capitol); however, the legislature continued to meet in the Grace Methodist Church in Harrisburg until 1906.

THE CIVIL WAR IN PENNSYLVANIA

Southeastern Pennsylvania first felt the full impact of the Civil War on October 9 and 10, 1862, when Jeb Stuart and his cavalry descended upon the town of Chambersburg in Franklin County. When they retreated on October 11, they took with them over 1,200 horses and approximately $150,000 worth of supplies, but the town had been spared—for the moment.

In the summer of 1863, Confederate troops again entered Pennsylvania under the command of Robert E. Lee as head of the Army of Northern Virginia. Various elements of their army were dispersed throughout the Adams, Franklin, and York counties of the state. The first to feel the reality of the war was York, which was entered by forces of General Early on June 26. The town surrendered to his forces the next day. While General Early demanded a ransom of $100,000 to alleviate any threat to the city, he received only $28,600, and his forces left the town on June 28.

Also in York County, Wrightsville felt the presence of the Confederates on June 28, when Confederate forces under General Gordon arrived to protect the wooden bridge over the Susquehanna River. The small force protecting the bridge was soon overpowered by the Confederates, but the defenders did succeed in burning the bridge.

Cumberland County also felt the full impact of the war, when on June 27 forces of General Ewell entered Carlisle, capturing the town without a fight. The presence of Confederate troops within twenty miles of Harrisburg, the state capital, caused great concern for Governor Curtin and the residents of that city.

All of the peripheral activity climaxed on July 1, when the Confederate army of 65,000 men met the Union army of 85,000 men in the small hamlet of Gettysburg, Adams County, with a population of fewer than three thousand citizens. The battle raged on for three days, and when it ended, the Union army losses in dead, wounded, and missing amounted to just over 23,000, while the Confederate losses amounted to over 20,000. The armies retreated, commencing on July 4, leaving a scene of horrible proportions both in human casualties as well as property damage for the people of Gettysburg to cope with. It should be noted that almost one-third of the Union army under General Meade at Gettysburg was composed of soldiers fighting for their home state of Pennsylvania.

Shortly after the battle, Governor Curtin visited the site and expressed concern about the handling of the dead soldiers. In response to his concern, two gentlemen of Gettysburg, David Wills and David McConnaughy, purchased seventeen acres of land on Cemetery Hill to establish a cemetery for the fallen Union soldiers at Gettysburg. The land was conveyed to the state, and soon William Saunders, a landscape artist, was commissioned to design the cemetery. In all, 3,500 unidentified Union soldiers were interred in the cemetery.

The Soldiers National Cemetery at Gettysburg became the first national cemetery and immediately became an attraction for Northern visitors. Some came to see where their loved ones had died, and some came simply to view the most famous Civil War battlefield in the North.

The initial date for the dedication of the cemetery was October 23, 1863, but it was shifted to November 19, 1863, due to the unavailability of the guest speaker, noted orator Edward Everett. President Lincoln was not invited to attend until November 2. Mr. Everett spoke for almost two hours, and his words are not remembered, while

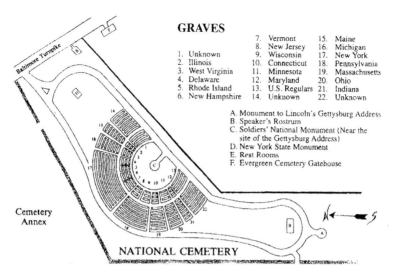

GRAVES

	7. Vermont	15. Maine
	8. New Jersey	16. Michigan
1. Unknown	9. Wisconsin	17. New York
2. Illinois	10. Connecticut	18. Pennsylvania
3. West Virginia	11. Minnesota	19. Massachusetts
4. Delaware	12. Maryland	20. Ohio
5. Rhode Island	13. U.S. Regulars	21. Indiana
6. New Hampshire	14. Unknown	22. Unknown

A. Monument to Lincoln's Gettysburg Address
B. Speaker's Rostrum
C. Soldiers' National Monument (Near the site of the Gettysburg Address)
D. New York State Monument
E. Rest Rooms
F. Evergreen Cemetery Gatehouse

Gettysburg National Cemetery

President Lincoln delivered what is now known as the Gettysburg Address in less than two minutes. That short speech has become a classic American presidential speech and contained the following words:

> *Now we are engaged in a great civil war, testing whether that nation, or any nation so conceived and so dedicated, can long endure. We are met on a great battle-field of that war. We have come to dedicate a portion of that field, as a final resting place for those who here gave their lives that this nation might live. It is altogether fitting and proper that we should do this.*

—Abraham Lincoln, November 19, 1863

The first state memorial to be placed on the Gettysburg battlefield was the First Minnesota Infantry Regiment's white marble urn placed in the cemetery in 1867. It remains there today.

The next year, 1864, Pennsylvania was once again to feel the presence of a Confederate force when on July 31 General McCausland once again occupied the town of Chambersburg. His raid was

First Minnesota Infantry marble urn.

in retaliation for Union General Hunter's raid into the Shenandoah Valley. McCausland demanded a ransom of $500,000 in currency or $100,000 in gold. The town could not raise the money and was burned by the Confederates. This disaster marks the last Confederate intrusion into Pennsylvania.

Spring of that same year saw the birth of what was to become the Gettysburg National Park: on April 30, 1864, the state chartered the Gettysburg Memorial Association to commemorate the battle, and by 1867, the state had started to procure land in the battlefield area. Soon, other states were helping in the purchase of land, and John Bachelder of Massachusetts was asked to write the authoritative history of the battlefield.

In a major event, on July 1–3, 1888, a Twenty-Fifth Anniversary of the Battle of Gettysburg was held, with many veterans of both sides in attendance. This was one year after the Pennsylvania Senate had appropriated $125,000 to mark the positions of the Pennsylvania commands on the battlefield. Finally on February 11, 1895, a bill sponsored by Representative Dan Sickles was passed establishing the Gettysburg battlefield as a national military park. It followed Chattanooga and Chickamauga as national military parks.

THE JOHNSTOWN FLOOD

Johnstown, located in the western part of the state, had known a relatively good period of economic growth in the 1880s. It was a town of predominately German and Welsh immigrants who worked in the local mines and in the Cambria Iron Works. Just above the town was Lake Conemuagh, which had been initially built to support the canal system—a system that soon ceased to operate. The lake had been created with an earthen dam known as the South Fork Dam.

After the canal period, the property had been purchased by a group of wealthy persons, including Andrew Carnegie, Henry Frick, and Andrew Mellon, to create a resort for their families, the South Fork Hunting and Fishing Club. After the purchase in 1879, they did some repairs to the earthen dam but chose to ignore many warnings about its stability.

On May 30, 1889, the area received over eight inches of rain in a twenty-four-hour period, and the pressure on the dam proved to be too much. At 3 p.m. on the afternoon of May 31, 1889, the dam broke, sending a thirty-six-foot wall of water (weighing more than fifty tons) down upon the town at a speed of fifty miles an hour. The results were disastrous: 2,209 persons were killed and 900 were missing (out of a population of 30,000), with the town sustaining over $18 million worth of property damage. The Cambria Iron Works alone—the first steel company in the United States to use Bessemer converters—suffered over a million dollars worth of damage. Within days of the flood, however, they had some of their furnaces active again.

Of the many stories of heroic actions during the flood, one in particular stands out. Mrs. Hettie Ogle was the Western Union telegraph operator in the town. She stayed at her post sending telegrams describing the flood until her death. The last telegram she sent simply said "This is my last message." And with that, Johnstown was cut off from the outside world. Mrs. Ogle died in the flood.

One of the first people to assist the victims after the flood was Clara Barton. She arrived under the Red Cross banner as one of the first relief agencies on the scene. Seeing the disaster, she quickly had lumber sent there to construct temporary shelters for the residents. After the flood relief effort, much of the lumber was sent to

Ruins of Johnstown after 1889 flood (looking up Stony Creek).

Washington to be used for the construction of a new Red Cross head-quarters building. When Miss Barton built her house in Glen Echo, Maryland, she specifically asked that some of the Johnstown lumber be used in the construction of her home. Today her home in Glen Echo, Maryland, survives—built predominately from wood that survived the great Johnstown flood.

After the flood, major debates arose concerning the causes of the dam breaking, many of which focused on the South Fork Hunting and Fishing Club. Many felt that the members of the club failed to respond to engineering reports of weaknesses in the dam. But it should be remembered that the rainfall that particular day was above the predictions for the hundred-year flood plain. To this day there is no clear resolution of the matter. The Johnstown flood is often cited as the most serious of natural disasters to strike the United States at that time.

Labor Issues

Conflicts between the eastern and western sections of the state paled in comparison with the conflicts between labor and management in Pennsylvania. Issues hotly debated included child labor, wages, working conditions, payment in company script, and discrimination against immigrants. The issues were real. As late as 1900, about 30 percent of Philadelphia's workforce was child labor, and in the coal fields about 15 percent of miners were boys under the age of fourteen. Workers were often expected to put in twelve hours per day, seven days a week, and payment was frequently in company script that could only be spent to pay for rent of a company-owned house or for food at the company store.

Throughout the period, various efforts were made to create labor unions to protect the rights of workers. Many flourished for a short period of time, such as the Workingmen's Benevolent Association founded in 1868. This association united the English, Irish, Scottish, and Welsh anthracite miners and did win some concessions for the miners, but between 1874 and 1875 it was successfully broken up by Franklin Gowen, acting president of the Philadelphia and Reading railroads. The struggle continued, and in 1897 the United Mine Workers Union was formed with John B. Rae of Pennsylvania as its first president.

Immigrants faced an "Alien Tax" passed by the state assembly that placed a three-cent-per-day tax on employers of aliens. The employers simply deducted the tax from the worker's salary. This tax, among other issues, led to the formation of what became known as the "Molly Maguires." This organization, whose membership consisted of Irish men, became viewed as a "semi-organized" group hostile to industrial leaders in their efforts to improve the working conditions of their fellow workers. The Maguires operated mainly in the Pennsylvania counties of Schuylkill, Carbon, Northumberland, Columbia, and Luzerne, and their tactics included the murdering of company officials.

Eventually the Maguires were infiltrated, members arrested, and the group disbanded. In 1876, several of the members were hanged after a conviction for murdering a company official. The Molly Maguires had a definite impact on the struggle between labor and management as they highlighted the abuses of labor management at a national level, thereby leading the way for change.

The conflicts often erupted into physical attacks and injury. Each of the three main industries of the state—railroads, steel, and

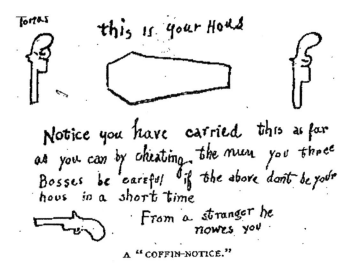

Facsimile of a Molly Maguire threatening note.

coal mining—felt the wrath of the workers. First to encounter labor problems were the railroads. In 1877, a strike erupted in Pittsburgh that had national consequences. The railroads had twice cut wages by 10 percent while at the same time increasing the size of the east-bound trains without a crew increase. A strike ensued in Pittsburgh that required the calling out of the National Guard. In the ensuing conflict, at least twenty strikers were killed and many wounded. The crowd then set fire to the roundhouse and other buildings, causing over $4 million worth of damage. In total they destroyed 39 buildings, 104 engines, 46 passenger cars, and 1,200 freight cars.

The steel industry did not escape the strikers' wrath. In the summer of 1892, the steelworkers at the Homestead plant, owned by Andrew Carnegie, went on strike. Negotiations broke down between management and the Amalgamated Association of Iron and Steel Workers. To prevent temporary workers, known as "scabs" (derivation unknown), from coming in and working, normally at lower wages, and effectively breaking the strike, the workers cordoned off the mill and would not allow the scab workers to enter. Frustrations rose and tempers flared. Frick, who was in charge of the plant for Carnegie, called in the Pinkerton Agency for assistance. Pinkerton agents, three hundred in number, arrived at the site to break the strikers' cordon and fighting erupted. Seven workers were killed and many wounded. The strike finally ended in November 1892, but it forever left a stain on the image of Andrew Carnegie as a friend of the working man.

Violence came to the mining industry in early September 1897, when the coal miners in the three counties of Luzerne, Carbon, and Schuylkill went out on strike. The neighboring Lattimer miners also wanted to strike, and they asked the Luzerne, Carbon, and Schuylkill strikers to march on their mine to support their leaving. On September 10, the march proceeded toward Lattimer but met with resistance from local authorities. Fighting occurred and shots were fired. In all, nineteen persons were killed, most of whom were of Slavic descent, and as many as fifty were wounded in the scuffle. The event became known as the Lattimer Massacre, and it became a symbol of the strife between labor and management.

Turbulent relations between labor and management continued throughout the late 1800s. It was not a "shining hour" for the state of Pennsylvania, but it was representative of the national issues involved in the growth of an industrial economy.

INDUSTRY

Agriculture

Agriculture continued to be a major industry throughout this period. Pennsylvania served as a major source of foodstuffs and horses for the Union troops during the Civil War. The main agricultural area in the state was the southwestern sector.

In the 1890s, locally grown fruit, which had previously been sold almost entirely inside the state, began to expand to a consumer market in states beyond Pennsylvania. Corn remained the most profitable money crop, and dairy farming rapidly became one of the major areas of concentration for farmers.

The raising of cattle diminished during the period as competition from the western states increased. However, horses continued to be raised and Pennsylvania became known on the national level for horse breeding. In 1890, there were more than 600,000 horses on farms within the state.

As the agricultural sector developed, becoming more a business and less a means for survival, the state, in 1895, established the Department of Agriculture to manage the various industrial issues that arose.

Coal

The coal industry in Pennsylvania flourished during the period, and while the state reacted to the labor-related violence frequently associated with the mines, it did little to ensure the safety of the miners as they worked. In 1865, the Pennsylvania General Assembly authorized the Coal and Iron Police to maintain order in the coal fields. These police became known to the miners as "Cossacks" or "yellow dogs." This was followed in 1868 by the establishment of the Department of Mines. Finally, in 1877, as a late response to a fire on September 6, 1868, at the Avondale mine where 108 men and boys were killed, the Bituminous Coal Mining Inspection Force was created by the general assembly and three mine inspectors appointed.

Demand for coal increased sharply by 1877, as all of the railroad engines were solely coal fueled. In addition, the steel industry began using coke in their refineries for the Bessemer process, thereby greatly increasing the demand. In the Connellsville region alone there were over 4,200 coke ovens producing coke for the steel industry.

Later in the period, various inventions were introduced that not only increased productivity but also improved the safety of the miners. A few of them are:

- The air-powered undercutting machine was invented in Chicago (1880).
- Charles Wolf invented the flame safety lamp, using naphtha for fuel instead of oil (1883). The lamp was developed for the purpose of detecting oxygen deficiencies and presence of methane gas.
- The first electric haulage motors were introduced into Pennsylvania mines (1887).

By the turn of the century the future of the coal industry in Pennsylvania appeared bright, as labor and management were more in accord, and it became established that almost all of the nation's anthracite coal was to be found in eight counties of the state: Schuylkill, Carbon, Luzerne, Northumberland, Lackawanna, Columbia, Dauphin, and Sullivan.

Electricity

Electricity, long identified with Benjamin Franklin, had another "first" in Pennsylvania in 1883, thanks to Thomas Edison and the invention of the light bulb. In 1870, Thomas Edison perfected the incandescent light bulb at his facility in Menlo Park, New Jersey. It was an immediate success for use in U.S. cities. Initially, in 1881, he constructed a power station on Pearl Street in New York City. The power was transmitted via underground cables. The underground cables proved to be very expensive and difficult to repair, and Edison soon developed what he called a "three-wire distribution system" that could be used above ground.

Edison had initial successes: in 1880, Philadelphia had electric street lights, and in 1881, John Wanamaker installed electric lights in his store in Philadelphia. Edison, however, wanted to demonstrate the effectiveness of his system for a small metropolitan area. His construction company began looking for likely locations to install such a power station. The criteria for selection consisted of a one-square-mile district, preferably a mix of residences and businesses; location of telegraph lines and trees so as not to interfere with the new lines; and adequate resources of coal and water to power the station.

One of the sites selected was in Sunbury, Pennsylvania, in the coal-mining region. Not only did it meet the local requirements, but a group of local financiers promised to fund the entire project. The Edison Construction Company installed the first three-wire distribution system in Sunbury and turned it on for the first time on July 4, 1883, thus making it one of the first towns in the United States to be totally lit by electricity.

Inventions

In 1874, Daniel Drawbaugh demonstrated his latest invention to the local citizens of Cumberland. His invention would later become known as the telephone. However, he did not file for a patent on the invention until 1880, due to lack of funds. Unfortunately for him, Alexander Bell filed his patent in 1876. Bell's claim to the invention of the telephone was upheld by the Supreme Court in October of 1887.

In Meadville in 1891, Whitcomb I. Judson invented a shoe fastener and formed the Hookless Fastener Company. What the company produced came to be known as the zipper, since it just "zipped" up the shoe. Earlier, in 1858, Hyman Lipman of Philadelphia created the pencil with an eraser, and in 1886 Theophilus van Kannel is credited with inventing the revolving door.

Lumber

Pennsylvania's dominance in the lumber trade came to an end around the year 1860, when the focus of the industry shifted first to Michigan and Wisconsin and later to the Pacific coastal states.

Merchandizing

In 1861, a young man by the name of John Wanamaker opened his first store in Philadelphia, called Oak Hall. In 1869, he opened his second, and finally in 1876, he consolidated all of his stores into the Grand Depot, which was built on the location of the old railroad station. His business boomed.

Wanamaker was a very progressive businessman, as is shown by the innovations employed in his stores:

> 1876–First U.S. store to show Paris and Berlin fashions; first store to send buyers abroad to foreign markets
> 1879–First full-page advertisement in a newspaper, making him the father of modern advertisement
> 1880–First use of pneumatic tubes for cashiers for the transfer of money

Wanamaker's Grand Depot department store

1881–Grand Depot lit by electricity
1882–First installation of elevators.

Another young entrepreneur, a Lancaster native named Milton Hershey, in 1886 established the Lancaster Caramel Company in Lancaster. The company flourished, and in 1894 Hershey added chocolate to his line. In 1900, Hershey sold the Caramel Company for $1 million but kept the chocolate part, for a new venture.

Oil

The presence of oil in the Oil Creek area of Pennsylvania had been a known fact since the days of the Indians. It was always considered to be a nuisance. This changed, and by 1858 petroleum was in high demand by the textile industry as a lubricant. One of the main sources of petroleum was an oil spring in the area near Titusville and Cornplanter in northwest Pennsylvania—an area purchased in 1854 by two businessmen, George H. Bissell and Jonathan G. Eveleth, on speculation. They formed the Pennsylvania Rock Oil Company of Connecticut, which morphed into the Seneca Oil Company in 1858. Edwin L. Drake was hired as the company's general agent.

Drake's first oil well.

Drake arrived in Titusville in 1858 and began his search for oil. His first effort was to dig a well at the site of the oil spring, but it collapsed. Drake then decided to drill a well, but this too collapsed due to ground water. Not to be defeated, Drake then decided to drive a thirty-two-foot cast iron pipe into the ground and drill inside the pipe. On August 27, 1859, oil was struck, and the oil industry in Pennsylvania was born. The first well produced eight to nineteen barrels of oil a day. By 1860, oil production in the area had increased to 500,000 barrels a day, and by 1861, over 2 million barrels of oil were produced daily.

Immediately, oil speculators arrived in the area and drilling abounded. A new town named Oil City soon became the center of activity, and by the late 1800s the Oil Exchange in Oil City controlled the world price of oil.

As the oil industry developed in Pennsylvania, investors were quick to respond. One of the first was John D. Rockefeller, who founded the Standard Oil Company of Pennsylvania in Pittsburgh in 1868. He quickly purchased other refineries and soon became the most powerful oil magnate in the state. By 1870, Standard Oil was the largest refinery in the entire world. The smaller refineries, in order to survive, consolidated to form the Pure Oil Company. Standard Oil literally allowed the Pure Oil Company to survive only by an agreement that the Pure Oil Company would not undersell Standard Oil. The Pure Oil Company endured for about fifty years.

Drake's achievement was not forgotten. In 1901, a monument was erected to him at Woodlawn Cemetery in Titusville, and his body was moved from Bethlehem to be interred by the monument.

Railroads

The earliest known railroad in Pennsylvania was constructed in 1810 in Delaware County. The purpose of the railroad was to transport quarry output, but by the beginning of the 1850s, the railroad network in the state had greatly expanded—largely to carry quarry and coal mine products to ports for transport. As the rail industry grew so did the associated manufacturers of items such as engines, railroad track, passenger cars, and railroad bridges.

As passenger travel increased, it became important to connect the western and eastern parts of the state via the railroad, and particularly to connect Philadelphia with Pittsburgh. Finally, in 1856, the connection was made, and with the new steam engines, travel time between the two cities decreased from three and a half days to only thirteen hours.

To achieve the linkage between Pittsburgh and Philadelphia, the engineers had to solve the problem of laying tracks on which trains could cross the Allegheny Mountains directly. John Edgar Thompson, an engineer, solved the problem in the Altoona area by constructing what came to be known as the "Horseshoe Curve." The construction

Horseshoe Curve

of the curve was completed on February 15, 1854. A true engineering feat to this day, the curve takes advantage of two ravines and literally goes around the high points to provide access to the western side of the Allegheny Mountains.

The main railroad force in the state at this time was the Pennsylvania Railroad, incorporated in 1847. By a system of purchasing smaller railroads and securing financial assistance, the Pennsylvania Railroad soon became the nation's largest railroad, with service to thirteen states and controlling 26,000 miles of track. Their railroads, by 1874, connected New York, Newark, Trenton, Philadelphia, Atlantic City, Wilmington, Baltimore, Washington, and Norfolk with Harrisburg, Pittsburgh, Buffalo, Erie, Cleveland, Columbus, Cincinnati, Louisville, Indianapolis, Chicago, and St. Louis.

Innovation came with the expansion of the railroads in the state. In 1869, George Westinghouse developed the air brake system, which he subsequently produced in his Westinghouse Air Brake Company in Pittsburgh. A few years later, Eli Janney patented the automatic safety knuckle buckle coupler, for the coupling of railroad cars. These couplers were also produced in Pittsburgh.

Some of the vestiges of the early railroad days in Pennsylvania are still very much a part of modern life. The phrase "stop, look, and listen" was first used on the Reading Railroad in 1884. And we still talk of the "Main Line" section of Philadelphia, which acquired its name from the Main Line of Public Works railroad that ran between Philadelphia and Malvern before going out of existence in 1857.

Shipbuilding

One does not think of Pittsburgh in terms of shipbuilding, but around 1860 shipbuilding in the state shifted from Philadelphia to Pittsburgh. The activity consisted predominately of constructing keel boats, flat boats, and steamboats, and lasted until about 1885, when it diminished.

Steel

By 1860, the production of iron products had replaced textiles as the number-one industry in Pennsylvania, with steel plants in the

Scranton and Phoenixville areas. With the commencement of the Civil War, the industry gained further prominence. In 1860, just prior to the war, the major ironworks of the state were:

> Thomas Iron Company and the Lehigh Crane Co., in Lehigh County
> Pennsylvania Iron Works, at Danville in Montour County
> Lackawanna Iron & Coal Company, at Scranton in Lackawanna County
> Phoenix Iron Company, at Phoenixville in Chester County
> Cambria Iron Company, at Johnstown in Cambria County

The iron industry exploded during the Civil War, with six new ironworks built in the Pittsburgh area in just one year. This increase led to iron and steel production worth over $18 million during the last eighteen months of the war.

Pig iron—iron produced from ore and formed into bars for later use—increased in production by 30 percent during the war years. By the end of the war, the state produced more than half of the total iron products for the entire country and six times that of any other state in the Union. Nine of the thirteen steel establishments in the United States were located in Pennsylvania, in both the western and eastern parts of the state.

At the time of the Civil War, these ironworks were in their infancy, and the United States imported virtually all of the steel it required from European sources. Steel, which is a strong alloy of iron and a carbon source, was in high demand. It was years after the Civil War, and as a result of their wartime efforts, that the Pennsylvania steel industry grew into a major contributor to the economy.

Over time, a group of men, including Andrew Carnegie, Henry Clay Frick, Eugene Grace, and Charles Schwab, began a series of consolidations and mergers that led to the emergence of three major steel companies in the state: Carnegie Steel Company, Bethlehem Steel Corporation, and the Cambria Iron Company.

Carnegie's interest in the steel business began in 1864, when he acquired an interest in a rolling mill to supply products to the railroads. Later, in 1872, he erected a Lucy furnace (named for his sister

Lucy), and with it he was one of the first to make Bessemer steel. Through a series of mergers and consolidations his holdings grew until, in 1900, the Carnegie Steel Company was incorporated, with capital in excess of $160 million. By this time, the Carnegie Corporation was producing one-fifth of all the pig iron and one-quarter of all the steel produced in this country. His expansion did not come without serious problems with his labor force.

The major problem occurred with the installation of the Bessemer furnaces in his plants. This new equipment greatly increased the efficiency of the process and, at the same time, decreased the required manpower. This conflict led to the violent Homestead Strike of 1892. The strike, called by the Amalgamated Association of Iron and Steel Workers (AA), proved to be detrimental to iron and steel union activities in Pennsylvania by pitting state militia and Pinkerton agents against the strikers, in what became outright conflict and received national attention. United States Secretary of War Henry Knox became involved. Finally, the strike was broken, but as a result the AA union faded into nonexistence, and by 1900 there were no iron or steel plants in the state with a union workforce.

Bethlehem Steel began in 1857 as Saucona Iron Works, becoming Bethlehem Iron Company in 1861 under the direction of John Fritz. In 1877, it became partial owner of the Bessemer patents, and by 1893 Bethlehem Iron was the largest ironworks in the world. That same year, the company was reorganized and renamed Bethlehem Steel Company.

The Cambria Iron Works was founded in Johnstown in 1854. By 1865, it was the largest ironworks in the United States. However, as other steel producers entered the steel-manufacturing area, the Cambria Works lost its edge and was reorganized in 1894 with a new name: the Cambria Steel Company. It was eventually sold to Bethlehem Steel in the 1920s.

Major technical advances in the production of iron and steel during the period include the following:

- 1855: The Bessemer converter was patented by John Bessemer. It greatly simplified the production of steel and was much less manpower intensive.

- 1857: William Kelly built a converter similar to the Bessemer converter at the Cambria Iron Works in Johnstown.
- 1859: Graff, Bennett & Co. used coke as fuel in the Clinton furnace, the first successful blast furnace in Pittsburgh. In 1860, they began using coke from the Connellsville region. This marks the beginning of the end for rural iron making.
- By 1864, 47 percent of all American pig iron had been smelted with anthracite. By 1880 that percentage had risen to over 56 percent.
- 1871: H. C. Frick borrowed $10,000 from Andrew Mellon to create 650 beehive coke ovens. Because money was scarce, Frick paid his workers with "Frick Dollars" redeemable only at his stores. Frick later merged with Carnegie.
- 1875: Andrew Carnegie established the first Bessemer steel plant—the Edgar Thompson Works in Braddock, Pennsylvania, to make steel rails.
- 1894: The Semett-Solvay Company builds the first byproduct coke ovens in the United States at Dunbar to capture tar, ammonia, oil, and gas waste from the beehive ovens.

By the end of the century the steel industry, primarily in the western part of Pennsylvania, had become the industrial giant of the state, thereby taking the lion's share of the focus off Philadelphia and moving it west to Pittsburgh.

Textiles

Throughout the latter half of the nineteenth century, Pennsylvania continued to be a leader in the manufacturing of textile products. In 1890, there were 79,500 persons involved in the industry, and the number continued to climb. The products produced included silk, woolens, knit goods, wool yarn, and worsteds (fabric that has been carded and spun prior to weaving). Textiles were at their peak, the second most important industry in the state.

In the mid-1800s the cotton industry flourished in Pennsylvania. In 1850, there were 105 cotton mills and 40 establishments for the dyeing and printing of cotton material. After the Civil War, this industry quickly faded to the South. However, the woolen industry continued unabated, growing from 270 factories in 1860 to 324 factories by 1880.

Another factor in textiles was the invention of the sewing machine in 1846, which led to a major change in the fabrication of clothing. Factories began to replace home industry, and by 1880 most clothing was made in factories. At this same time, a migration of silk mills took place into the state from New York and New Jersey. The mills moved, in general, to the coal-mining areas of Pennsylvania, such as the Schuylkill, Lehigh, and Susquehanna valleys. These areas provided many women and children who could work in the mills.

In addition to manufacturing textiles to be later made into clothing, Pennsylvania had long been a center for the manufacturing of hats. That industry got a boost in 1865 when John Batterson Stetson, from New Jersey, arrived in Philadelphia and, with no capital to speak of, started a hat business. His enterprise became world famous as the maker of the Stetson cowboy hat, and it grew to be the largest hat manufacturer in the world.

The late 1800s also saw continued growth in carpet manufacturing, as Pennsylvania became the carpet and rug center of the nation. In 1850, the state ranked third in carpet production with products valued at 21 percent of the national output. By 1870, the state ranked first in carpet production with a 45 percent share of the market, and by 1900, that share had grown to 48 percent. After the turn of the century, this industry went into a decline due mainly to the higher wages paid in the state and the shortage of local wool.

People

The population of the state of Pennsylvania in 1850 was 2.3 million persons. By 1900, that number had grown to 6.3 million residents. The growth began early on, and by the time of the Civil War, the state was populated in all areas. This is when the population began to shift to the urban centers, particularly Philadelphia and Pittsburgh. Philadelphia's population had grown from 121,376 in 1850 to 1.3 million in 1900 (partially due to annexation), making it the third largest city in the United States. For Pittsburgh, the growth was even greater. In 1850, it had 46,000 residents, and by 1900 that number had grown to 321,000, making Pittsburgh the eleventh largest city in the United States.

By 1900, 2.3 percent of the total population of the state was African American; however, in Philadelphia, African Americans represented 5 percent of the total population. General immigration continued, with a shift of countries of origin for the immigrants. Initially the immigrants had come from Western European countries such as England, Germany, France, and Ireland. In this later period (1850–1900), however, the immigrants were increasingly from Slavic countries, Italy, Scandinavia, and Finland. Many of the immigrants were Jewish.

With the advent of the Civil War, women began to take a more prominent role in American society. Many went to work to support their families, while others took up causes such as the abolition of slavery. Philadelphia became a center for women's rights and other issues. The first Women's Medical College opened in Philadelphia in 1850, and eleven years later the Philadelphia Hospital opened the first nursing school in the United States.

The new immigrants tended to settle where the work was, and this frequently meant either in coal-mining areas or steel-production sites. Many of the small towns that grew up around these facilities were concentrations of a specific ethnic group, where they continued to speak the language and maintain the customs of their native lands. The state became an ethnic quilt composed of many subcultures.

The influx of African Americans into the state had begun prior to the Civil War and gained momentum after the war ended. As they settled in and began looking for work, an unusual association arose: it was a trade guild for caterers, and it became very successful. The guild would search out new arrivals and train them to work for them as waiters, initially as house servants and later as independent caterers. Some of the early successful caterers were Bogle, Augustin, Prosser, Jones, and Mintou. Others used the skills they had learned as slaves, such as boot making and blacksmithing, to establish their own businesses.

The African Americans in the state sought freedom from the discrimination of the South but found it only in a piecemeal fashion. The state legislature and the state supreme court played a major role in the adjustment. Some of the major actions were as follows:

1854 (May 8): The Act for the Regulation and Continuance of a System of Education by Common Schools was enacted. The act required that the various school districts in the state establish separate schools for "Negro and Mulatto children." In districts where these schools were established, the district was not compelled to admit such pupils to any other school.

1863 (March 6): A petition was circulated in the legislature proposing to ban immigration of freedmen to Pennsylvania. The petition was denied by the Senate Committee on Legislation.

1867: In the case before the Supreme Court of Pennsylvania of *West Chester and Philadelphia Company v. Miles*, the court decided that "separation of Negroes to assigned seats for good order" was not illegal for railways or other modes of transportation.

1867 (March): The same year as the supreme court decision in the *Miles* case, the legislature overturned the decision by enacting legislation that stated that "Negroes were to have the same rights on railways etc. as whites."

1870 (April 17): The state legislature enacted a law repealing the previous acts that only white freemen had the right to vote. All freemen, without distinction of color, now had the right to vote.

1874: A new state constitution removed all restrictions for voting based on color.

1874 (April 10): The Pennsylvania Supreme Court awarded damages to African Americans who were ejected from a theater (*Drew v. Peer*).

1878 (March 15): The Pennsylvania Supreme Court awarded damages to Mr. and Mrs. Green from the Central Railroad of New Jersey, for compelling them to move from one railway car to another specifically because of the color of their skin.

1881 (June 8): The legislature passed an act titled Mixed Schools, which stated, "It shall be unlawful for any school director, superintendent, or teacher to make any distinction whatever on account of, or by reason of, the race or color of any pupil or scholar who may be in attendance upon or seeking admission to any public or common school maintained wholly on or in part under the school laws of the Commonwealth." This act resulted from a lawsuit filed in 1881 by Elias H. Allen of Meadville, who sued to have his children admitted to a white school in their neighborhood.

1887 (May 19): The legislature passed the Act to Provide Civil Rights for all People, Regardless of Race or Color. The act stated that "any person, company, corporation, being owner, lessee or manager of any restaurant, hotel, railroad, street railway, omnibus line, theatre, concert hall, or place of entertainment or amusement, who shall refuse to accommodate, convey, or admit any person or persons account of race or color over their lines or into their hotel, restaurant, theatre, concert hall or place of amusement, shall upon conviction thereof be guilty of a misdemeanor punished by a fine of not less than fifty or more than one hundred dollars."

1895 (July 2): The Life Insurance Act was passed, which stated that life insurance companies were not allowed to discriminate as to premiums, dividends, or otherwise, between insured of the same class and expectation of life.

So while African Americans continued to migrate to Pennsylvania, their lives continued to be a struggle. The state, however, through a long series of legislation and court actions, did make great strides during this period to alleviate any discrimination against any person regardless of color.

Arts and Culture

Between 1850 and 1900, the arts continued to flourish in Pennsylvania. Prior to the Civil War, Philadelphia was the leading publisher of magazines in the entire country and had become known as "Magazine City." But many of the magazines ceased publication around the time of the Civil War due to shortages of labor and resources.

In the world of painting, the state was also well represented with such luminaries as Charles Rembrandt Peale, Thomas Sully, John Neagle, Thomas Eakins, Edwin Austin Abbey, and Mary Cassatt. There were a great number of sculptors as well, including John Boyle, Charles Grafly, Joseph A. Bailly, and, arguably Pennsylvania's best sculptor, George G. Barnard. In both of these artistic areas, the emphasis shifted from the portraiture of the wealthy to more depictions of the average man and his environment.

The presence of music had always been an active part of the cultural scene of Pennsylvania. Of particular importance was the founding of the Germania Orchestra Society of Philadelphia in 1856, the later founding of the Pittsburgh Symphony in 1896 with Frederick Archer as the conductor, and the founding of the Philadelphia Symphony in 1900, conducted by Fritz Scheel. In 1898, Victor Herbert became conductor of his own orchestra. And among composers, Stephen Foster is well remembered for works such as *Oh Susanna* and *Old Folks at Home*.

Andrew Carnegie donated a magnificent concert hall to Pittsburgh, which included a grand organ. Organ recitals are frequent events in Pittsburgh to this day. Philadelphia, however, remained the theatrical center, dominated by the acting families of Drew and Barrymore.

Pennsylvania luminaries were also rising in the field of literature. Poet Stephen Vincent Benet authored *John Brown's Body*, Owen Wister wrote *The Virginian*, and Louisa Mae Alcott penned *Little Women*.

THE INDIANS

While it is safe to say that by 1850 the Indian population in Pennsylvania was miniscule, in 1879, the Indian Industrial School opened in the quiet town of Carlisle. Richard Henry Pratt, a U.S. Army officer who spent eight years in Indian Territory as the commander of an African American "Buffalo Soldier" cavalry unit, had a theory about American Indians. He was convinced that if you took the children away from their tribes and in his own words "killed the Indian and saved the man," they would assimilate into "normal" society and become participating citizens. Pratt pushed the idea for years, and finally in 1879, he received permission from Secretary of the Interior Schurz and Secretary of War McCary to use the deserted army base known as Carlisle Barracks in Carlisle, Pennsylvania, for what became known as the Indian Industrial School. It was the first Indian boarding school in the country. By 1899, there were twenty-five such schools located in fifteen states. Originally meant for Indian students, they later also included students from the Philippines and Puerto Rico.

The initial students, both boys and girls, were recruited from the various Indian tribes and transported to Carlisle. The first students arrived on October 6, 1879. The transition to "white man ways" was immediate, as their hair was cut, shoes were required, and no one was allowed to speak his or her native language—only English would be spoken. This treatment was severe as, for many Indians, their hair was a sign of their manhood and its loss a matter of shame.

The original group consisted of eighty-two students, but over the years of the school's operation (from 1879 until 1918) the number of students rose to over one thousand per year. The curriculum was a combination of academic studies such as history, English, mathematics, and science for half a day and vocational studies the other half. For the boys, those studies centered on agriculture or mechanical trades, while the girls were taught to be dressmakers, cooks, laundresses, or other domestic professions. The school was also known for the high caliber of its football team. In total, over ten thousand students attended the school; however, only about one thousand actually graduated.

Ton Torlino, of the Navajo tribe, just prior to and just after entering the Carlisle Indian School.

Student Body assembled on the Carlisle Indian School grounds.

An Indian student's grave.

129

During the summer months, the Indian children did not return to their native tribes but, using a program called "Outgoing," were hired out to local families to work as servants in their homes. Frequently, the conditions of their servitude were not entirely favorable. The families often viewed the Indians merely as a source of labor and did little to encourage them in their adjustments to their new lives.

The basic premise was that the students, once "educated," would not return to their tribes upon completion of their schooling but integrate into mainstream, white society. This did not happen, as most of the students returned to their native tribes, where they found that readjustment was very difficult. Many no longer spoke their native language and found it difficult to find a job, either on the reservation or outside. However, the Carlisle Indian Industrial School survived until 1918 when it finally closed its doors, like many of the other Indian boarding schools around the country. The Indian Industrial School remains a major element in the local history of Carlisle.

The late 1800s ended with abated conflicts internal to the state but with an impending conflict arising on the international scene. The state had become a unified entity due to the Civil War, and the industries of the state had emerged as national leaders in their particular areas. The population was now a true mix of ethnic groups, all of which contributed to the vitality of the state. While no longer a Quaker state, Pennsylvania still held to many of the Quaker ideals, as exemplified by the nickname of Philadelphia: the City of Brotherly Love. The residents of Pennsylvania were introspective in their attitude toward the rest of the world. They paid little attention to the storm clouds gathering in Europe—the same clouds that would soon darken their peaceful image of the world around them.

Chapter Eight

War and Peace

(1900–1950)

General History

The period from 1900 to 1950 was one of extremes. It began with the cessation of hostilities of the Spanish-American War—that treaty was signed in Paris in 1899—and was followed by the ending of hostilities in the Philippines in 1903. But the peace did not last long: less than twenty years later the United States became involved in the conflict in Europe later known as World War I. The action was hotly contested by isolationist groups in the United States such as the American Neutrality League. The war was a difficult time for many Pennsylvanians of German descent, and they were often looked upon with suspicion. Many no longer spoke their native language of German, and others anglicized their names to be less conspicuous.

After the war ended, the national interest focused on faltering economic growth and the growing strength of the labor movement. Labor conditions continued to be one of the major issues of the time, especially in industrial states such as Pennsylvania. However, all of these concerns faded in 1929 with the advent of the Great Depression. The impact of the Depression was felt throughout the entire 1930 decade, with many families suffering complete devastation— loss of homes, jobs, and financial savings. The Pennsylvania economy had previously been strong and insulated from economic downturns. While the agricultural area was able to produce commodities for personal use as well as for the marketplace, the industrial sector suffered greatly.

At the same time, war was once again looming on the horizon in Europe. And again, the isolationist movement was very strong throughout the country—until December 7, 1941, when the Japanese attacked the U.S. Navy at Pearl Harbor. This attack led to the United States declaring war on the Axis powers of Germany, Japan, and Italy.

The U.S. entry into the war relieved, to a large extent, the unemployment problems in the states. Manufacturing flourished, and, along with the other manufacturing states, Pennsylvania regained its industrial strength. The U.S. residents of German, Italian, and Japanese descent quickly united behind the federal government.

The first half of the twentieth century ended on a relatively peaceful note. But now the United States knew that for the foreseeable future they would be a leader on the world stage—a new phenomenon for the country and the individual states.

During the period, the United States also experienced a definite population shift from the east to the more western states. This shift is reflected in the distribution of seats in the U.S. House of Representatives. In 1910, the Pennsylvania delegation represented 12 percent of the House of Representatives; by 1950, that percentage had dropped to 6.5 percent. The population was shifting, and so were the various state political power bases.

The post–World War II environment focused on such issues as re-assimilation of veterans back into their civilian lives, adjustment to the U.S. role on the international stage, and predominately internal matters.

All of this changed on June 25, 1950, when the Democratic People's Republic of Korea (DPRK) crossed the 38th parallel and invaded their neighbor to the south, the Republic of Korea (ROK)—the Korean War had started. This event was looked upon as part of the Soviet plan for world domination that was developing at the same time, and the ensuing standoff between the United States and the U.S.S.R. became known as the Cold War.

NATIONAL

Labor and labor issues within Pennsylvania frequently gained national attention. A good example is the anthracite coal strikes of 1900 and

1902, which involved over 150,000 coal miners. The strike in 1900 did not end on a satisfactory note, as management refused to recognize the union. This led to the strike in 1902, which lasted five months. Negotiations to solve the issues remained stalemated until President Theodore Roosevelt focused national attention on the strike's impasse and intervened by calling all parties to a negotiation session. When negotiations failed, President Roosevelt threatened to call out the U.S. Army to run the mines, along with the Pennsylvania Militia that was already there. A commission was established, and all sides agreed to abide by their decision, which came in October 1902. While the miners received a small pay raise and a reduction of hours, their primary issue of the official recognition of their union— the United Mine Workers—as the miners negotiating agent was not acknowledged by the mine owners. This set the tone for the future, as strikes became more frequent. Finally, in 1933, the United Mine Workers achieved the right of collective bargaining for the mining industry. This strike is the first strike in the United States in which the president did not side with the owners but tried to negotiate a settlement. All unions throughout the country watched these events closely.

In 1901, the keel was laid for the second U.S. naval vessel to carry the name *Pennsylvania*. The ship, classed as an Armored Cruiser No. 4, was launched on August 22, 1903, when it joined the fleet. On January 18, 1911, a plane flown by Eugene Ely landed on a platform constructed on the ship. Later, on August 27, 1912, the ship was renamed the *Pittsburgh* to free the name *Pennsylvania* for a new battleship. The *Pittsburgh* remained on active duty until July 1931, when it was sold for scrap.

In October 1913, the keel was laid for the next U.S. Navy ship to be named the *Pennsylvania*. It was launched on March 16, 1915, and joined the fleet in 1916. This *Pennsylvania* became one of the ships damaged by the Japanese attack on Pearl Harbor on December 7, 1941. It was taken back to the mainland, repaired, and rejoined the fleet in March of 1942. It served all of World War II in the Pacific theater and later met an unfortunate demise. It became one of the target ships for the atomic bomb tests at Bikini Atoll during

First aircraft to land on a vessel—USS Pennsylvania, *1911 (later the USS* Pittsburgh*).*

USS Pennsylvania *(1934)*

1946. It was finally sunk off Kwajalein Lagoon in February 1948. In its day it had been the largest battleship in the world.

As the war clouds gathered over Europe, they were also gathering in the United States over the question of liquor. It finally came to a head on December 18, 1917, when the U.S. Congress passed the Eighteenth Amendment banning all liquor production and consumption in the United States. The amendment was then sent to the states for their ratification. Pennsylvania, with a large German population accustomed to drinking beer, faced a dilemma. At that time, there were over eighty-five breweries operating in the state, all of which would be out of business if the amendment passed. After a long delay, Pennsylvania approved the amendment on February 21, 1919—about a month after the amendment had already become law. One of the breweries, the Yuengling Brewery, established in 1829, went into the production of ice cream as well as "near" beer (less than 1.5 percent alcohol by volume).

When World War I broke out in Europe, the German immigrants in Pennsylvania faced a serious problem. They wanted to be seen as American and not German. To counter the anti-German feelings, many residents of Germanic descent "Americanized" their names and spoke the German language only in their homes. Even when the United States entered the war, Germans were still suspect, since organizations such as the German-American Alliance were active in their support of Germany. Actions were taken to include the barring of instruction in German language in the public schools, and the Philadelphia Symphony Orchestra refused to play any music composed by any German composer.

At the same time, there was in the state a strong movement for pacifism, sponsored by such organizations as the Socialists and the Industrial Workers of the World, as well as the American Neutrality League, active in Philadelphia. All this changed when the United States actually entered the war in April of 1917.

The state "turned to" once the United States was in the war, and differences were forgotten for a common cause. A total of 324,299 Pennsylvanians joined the U.S. Army, 45,927 the U.S. Marines, and 735 the U.S. Coast Guard. This represented 7.79% of the entire military services at the time. In addition, the state subscribed enthusiastically to Liberty Bonds, purchasing a total of $2,709,800.

Being an industrial state, a large portion of the military supplies were manufactured within Pennsylvania, with over 2,372 manufacturers contributing to the cause. The world's largest shipyard was built in the Philadelphia area on what was known as Hog Island. The shipyard did not come online in time to provide ships for the war effort (as the first ship was launched in April 1918), but later it did produce over 120 ships, many of which were cargo ships that saw action in World War II. The ships were distinctive in design and became known as "Hogislanders." The site of the Hog Island Shipyard is now the Philadelphia airport.

Not long after the war, the Nineteenth Constitutional Amendment was passed by Congress on June 4, 1919, providing voting rights for all women. Unlike the Eighteenth Amendment, it was ratified by the Pennsylvania legislature just three weeks later on June 24, 1919, and it became the law of the land on August 18, 1919. It should be noted, however, that in 1913, the Pennsylvania legislature passed an amendment to the state constitution allowing women the right to vote, but the male voters in the state rejected the proposed amendment.

The Eighteenth Amendment ban on alcohol was defiantly ignored in both Philadelphia and Pittsburgh. They both became known as two of the "wettest" cities in the country, partially because of the inactivity of the state legislature. That body failed to pass two of the three enforcement proposals of Governor Pinchot and failed to fund the one Enforcement Act passed. Individuals were more subservient to the Eighteenth Amendment, but "bathtub" gin became very popular as well as homemade wine. This all changed again in 1933 when the Twenty-first Amendment to the Constitution was passed by the U.S. Congress. That amendment voided the Eighteenth Amendment and once again made the use and sale of alcohol products legal. The Yuengling Brewery celebrated by producing a new beer called Winner and sent a truckload of the new beer to President Roosevelt.

Winner beer poster

After World War I, Pennsylvania, like the rest of the United States, experienced what came to be known as the Roaring Twenties. It was a time for the women of the state to enjoy a new sense of freedom in their lifestyles and their dress as well as their attitude. Women began to wear short skirts, bob their hair, and create an image that became known as the "flapper." They were revolting against strict Victorian rules and conservatism. Life was light and gay with few worries. Both Pittsburgh and Philadelphia became centers of influence for the flapper generation.

The roaring 1920s came to a collapse with the Great Depression of 1929. Pennsylvania represented 8 percent of the national population, but the state unemployment stood at 10 percent. Most of the unemployment assistance was privately funded and not adequate. Governor Pinchot called several special sessions of the legislature to enact legislation to assist the workers, but nothing happened. Finally, in 1934, the federal Works Projects Administration (WPA) threatened to cut off all their funds to Pennsylvania unless state action was taken to provide assistance to needy workers in the state. The state legislature buckled under the pressure of the WPA, passing a bill providing for $20 million of assistance to help the struggling labor force in the state.

On July 3, 1938, the town of Gettysburg once again took the national spotlight as President Franklin Roosevelt dedicated the Eternal Light Peace Memorial on the Gettysburg Battlefield, marking the seventy-fifth anniversary of the battle. The monument was designed by Paul Phillippe Cret, with sculptures by Lee Lawrie. The $60,000 project was funded by the states of Wisconsin, Virginia, New York, Indiana, Tennessee, Illinois, and Pennsylvania. The shaft of the monument is Alabama Rockwood limestone and the pavements are Crab Orchard flagstone from Tennessee.

The inscriptions on the monument are as follows:

> At the bottom of the shaft:
> *"Peace Eternal in a Nation United"*

> And on a side panel:
> *To the Memory of*
> *Every man, woman and child who*
> *Participated in anyway in the*
> *Conflict of 1861 to 1865*

Eternal Light Peace Memorial, Gettysburg

Of the 12,000 Civil War veterans surviving at the time, over 1,300 Union veterans and almost 500 Confederate veterans attended the dedication of the monument by President Roosevelt. The federal government provided free transportation by special trains and buses for all the veterans. Each veteran was also provided with an attendant who accompanied him for the entire trip. In addition to the veterans, it is estimated that 250,000 civilians attended the ceremony. The 1938 reunion was the last for the Civil War veterans.

Confederacy meets Union

Massive crowd at dedication

On December 7, 1941, world events necessitated a major change in both the federal and state governments. We were once again at war, and once again citizens were asked to defend the country. The industrial complex swung into full gear. Pennsylvania supplied 1,250,000 men and women for the armed forces, to include: 667,000 men and 12,000 women in the army; 249,026 men and 7,444 women in the navy/marines; 39,466 men and 1,500 women in the Army Air Corps; and 11,600 men and 843 women in the Coast Guard. Of this total, there were 33,057 members killed in action and 65,106 wounded in action. Thirty-five servicemen from Pennsylvania received the Congressional Medal of Honor (the highest total of any state), and the state provided 189 army generals, 4 marine generals, and 10 admirals.

In addition, in support of the war effort, the former Indian School at Carlisle became the Army Medical Field Service School, graduating 27,853 medical doctors who served with the armed forces.

Industry also met the challenge. There were eight hundred plants in the state involved in war production. Actual production in 1939 was $5 billion, and in 1944 it had risen to $15 billion. Steel production in 1945 in the State amounted to 28,675,963 tons of steel. This represented one-third of the entire steel production in the country and 20 percent of the entire world production. Some of the major contributors to the war effort were the following:

- Westinghouse Corporation developed a wakeless, electrically powered torpedo.
- Hershey Chocolate Corporation developed the D-ration for the troops.
- The Bantam Car Company of Butler developed the prototype Jeep.
- Mack truck produced heavy-duty trucks and half-tracks for the army.
- The Baldwin Locomotive Works in Philadelphia produced tanks.

*Prototype of Bantam Car
Company Jeep*

In addition to the manufacturing side of the state, the agricultural side also made a major contribution, as shown below:

	1941	1945
Chickens	30 M	41 M
Turkeys	900 K	1.6 M
Eggs	172 M (dozens)	232 M (dozens)
Milk	435 K (gallons)	610 K (gallons)
Income (earned)	$280 M	$675 M

However, during World War II, strikes in Pennsylvania got national attention. In 1943, the Federal Fair Employment Practices Commission ordered the Philadelphia Transportation system to hire African American conductors and motormen on buses and trolleys. On August 11, 1943, the day the new employees were to report, the union, opposed to the new African American employees, struck, causing a complete shutdown of the buses and trolleys. President Roosevelt intervened and sent six thousand federal troops to the city to run the buses and trolleys. He also informed the strikers that if they continued the strike they would lose their deferments.

Postwar, the industrial base of the state remained solid and the residents prospered. Like most of the states, Pennsylvania was focused on issues related to the state's industrial/labor problems and the re-assimilation of its returning veterans into society—national interests came second.

The Korean War, which began on June 25, 1950, changed all that once again for Pennsylvania. Once again the state was called upon to provide men for the armed forces and military priorities came to the forefront for industry.

INTERNAL

At the turn of the century, the state legislature was still meeting in the Grace United Methodist Church, waiting for their new capitol. In 1899, architect Henry I. Cobb of Chicago had received approval to build a new capitol at a cost of $550,000. However, early in the construction, it was decided that the proposed new building was not suitable, and the project was dropped.

In 1901, the state legislature moved to stop construction on the Cobb Building and have a new design competition. One of the major criteria placed on the firms interested in bidding was that the architect had to be a Pennsylvanian, thus eliminating Cobb from the competition. The new winner was Joseph M. Huston, who incorporated the walls of the Cobb building into his design.

Cobb Capitol Building

Huston's state capitol building in Harrisburg

House Chamber

Senate Chamber

Construction began on the new capitol with the laying of the cornerstone on May 5, 1904, and it was officially dedicated on October 4, 1906, by President Theodore Roosevelt, who remarked at the ceremony that the new building was "the most beautiful State Capitol in the nation."

Problems soon arose, as the authorized funding for the new building by the legislature was $4 million and the actual cost for the building and the furnishings amounted to over $12 million. When governor-elect Edwin S. Stuart replaced Governor Samuel W. Pennypacker, both Republicans, things began to fall apart. The new state treasurer uncovered a huge scandal involving the funds for the new building. The scandal involved cost overruns, bribes, and corruption. For instance, the cost of the bootblack stand was found to have an actual cost of $125, while the state was charged $1,619.20.

After a complete investigation, six of the men involved in the building project were charged, tried, and convicted. They all served time in jail—with the exception of the ex–state treasurer, who died of natural causes several days after the sentencing. Former governor Pennypacker was not implicated in the scandal.

BOOTBLACK STAND, COST $1519.20,
18285 State Capitol, Harrisburg, Pa.

Bootblack stand

While the legislature met in their off-site location, they continued to function. Labor disputes remained the main issue of the day and would remain so for many years. Legislative actions taken while the capitol building was being completed reflect this concern. In 1903, the general assembly passed an act raising the minimum age for children working in factories and mines to fourteen and banned night work for children. In 1909, the Department of Factory Inspection was created, and it began to enforce the law limiting children's work hours to no more than ten hours a day. Child labor remained an issue in Pennsylvania until 1913, when a child's work hours were limited to no more than fifty-four hours a week.

Between 1900 and 1910, as the state population began to decrease due to the decline in industrial jobs, Pennsylvania experienced the largest influx of immigrants of any decade in its history. The European immigrants came mostly from Slavic countries, Italy, Finland, and the Scandinavian countries. Later, World War I curtailed European immigration, but African Americans were moving north. In Philadelphia alone, the African American population rose from 83,000 in

1910 to 134,000 in 1920. By World War II, 5 percent of the state population was African American. These waves of immigration were due to the fact that jobs were available in the state and the standard of living was much higher in Pennsylvania.

The arrival of African Americans was not met with favor in some parts of the state. In 1911 in the town of Coatesville, Zachariah Walker, an African American, in a drunken rage struggled with a policeman and subsequently killed him. When apprehended, he shot himself in the jaw in a suicide attempt. Taken to a hospital, a mob soon arrived, abducted him, built a bonfire outside of town, and burnt Walker alive. To his dying days he declared that he had shot the policeman in self-defense. As a result of this action, anti-lynching legislation was introduced, but it was not until 12 years later, in 1923, under Governor Pinchot, that it was enacted.

The increase of African American citizens in Pennsylvania is often unfairly blamed for several problems, including race riots in Philadelphia in June 1918 and the arrival of the Ku Klux Klan in Pennsylvania, who by 1920 had a membership of twenty thousand in the state. The "Great Migration" also led to the development of a distinct Philadelphia African American culture, including an African American newspaper (the *Philadelphia Tribune*), the founding of the African American Methodist Episcopal Church (AME) in Philadelphia, and one of the first African American representatives in the state House of Representatives, John C. Asbury, introducing an equal rights bill in 1921. The bill passed the house but not the senate. A new equal rights bill was not introduced and passed by the Pennsylvania state legislature until 1938. The later bill banned racial discrimination in hotels, restaurants, and places of public amusement.

In October 1918, the Spanish flu epidemic hit the state. There were more deaths in Philadelphia than in any other major city in the country. The total flu-associated deaths for the state amounted to thirteen thousand, with a one-day total of over seven hundred deaths.

The population of the state, already in a decline, received a major setback in October 1929, when the Great Depression began throughout the United States. By 1937, the state had almost 1.4 million, or 17.1 percent, of the workforce unemployed. This was partially the result of industrial production dropping to about one-half of what it had been in 1929. In addition, personal income had fallen from $775 in 1929 to $321 per year by 1941.

Financial assistance to the unemployed was generally privately funded until 1932, when the private sector could no longer support its charitable role. Finally, Governor Pinchot called for a special session of the legislature to address the problem, but little happened during these sessions. Ultimately, the federal government interceded with the New Deal Act to assist the unemployed. However, the state legislature still languished on the problem of financial support of the unemployed. It was not until 1934, when the federal government threatened to cut off their federal aid, that the Pennsylvania state legislature reacted and provided $20 million to assist the needy.

During this same time, Governor Pinchot tried to get the legislature to enact assistance for the laboring class. He wanted mandatory unemployment insurance, minimum wages for women and minors, maximum hours for workers, prohibition of child labor, and pensions for the elderly. Virtually nothing happened on the legislative front. The problem remained, and by 1938, the unemployment figure had risen to 1,454,000 persons, or approximately 18 percent of the state's population. The beginning of World War II created many new jobs and alleviated the unemployment problem for Pennsylvania.

In the post–World War II period, labor unions and management continued in a combative mode with one another, leading to a great deal of turmoil for the workers in the state. Along with labor issues, other social issues came to the forefront, such as the equal rights movement, equal education for all classes and races, and a voice in government for all citizens. These social issues were common to all of the states, and each state handled them in their own manner.

ARTS AND CULTURE

In 1937, at the request of an endowment from Andrew W. Mellon, a native Pennsylvanian, the National Gallery of Art was founded in Washington, D.C. When the building opened on March 17, 1941, the collection was mainly composed of gifts from the five founding benefactors, four of whom were from Pennsylvania—Andrew W. Mellon, Samuel H. Kress, Peter A. B. Widener, and Lessing J. Rosenwald. The fifth benefactor was Chester Dale from New York.

CATASTROPHIC EVENTS

Even after the Johnstown flood of 1889, problems with frequency of flooding in Pennsylvania remained. In 1911, the small town of Austin on the Allegheny River in Potter County experienced the same fate as Johnstown. The dam above the town built by the Bayliss Pulp and Paper Company broke and literally destroyed the town. Seventy-eight of the town's 2,200 residents were killed, and the damage was estimated to be over $5 million.

The Austin flood was followed by more widespread flooding on March 17, 1936, when Pittsburgh, Johnstown, Steelton, and Brackenridge were all inundated. This flood caused over $50 million worth of property damage and led to the Flood Control Act of 1936 and the establishment of the LFPP (Local Flood Protection Program). The LFPP and the Army Corps of Engineers greatly assisted the flood-prone areas by redirecting streams and constructing dams.

Flooding was not the only catastrophic event to hit the state during the period. On October 19, 1948, the town of Donora in Washington County was suddenly enveloped in thick smog that lasted for three days. The town, located in the Monongahela River valley, was the home of the Donora Zinc Works and the American Steel and Wire Company, both owned by the U.S. Steel Corporation. On that day, a temperature inversion caused all the fumes coming from the plants to fall rather than rise. The smog, composed of sulfur dioxide, carbon monoxide, and metal dust, caused the death of twenty residents and made over six thousand residents seriously ill. The tragedy at Donora led the state to enact the Clean Air Act in 1955 in an attempt to prevent the incident from happening again.

The coal-mining industry experienced its share of catastrophes. The highest number of accident victims in the state's history occurred

Noontime during the Donora smog disaster, 1948.

in 1907. A total of 1,514 miners were killed in one year—708 in the anthracite mines and 806 in the bituminous mines. Other major mine disasters included these:

1902	Rolling Mill Mine	Explosion killed 112 miners
1904	Harwick Mine	Explosion killed 179 miners
1908	Rachel & Agnes Mine	Mine explosion killed 154 miners
1928	Mather Mine Nr. 1	Explosion killed 195 miners

Coal mining continued to be a very dangerous profession.

LABOR ISSUES

Labor issues during the period focused on the formation of unions, child labor, female workers, salaries, benefits for the workers, and the gradual decline of manufacturing output in the state. There were two main unions at the time: the Congress of Industrial Organizations (CIO) and the American Federation of Labor (AFL). However, there were also unions specific to particular crafts, such as the United Textile Workers of America (founded in 1901), the United Mine Workers (founded in 1890 in Ohio), and the Steel Workers Organizational Committee (1930s), which in 1942 became the United Steel Workers of America. All of these unions pressured industry for better benefits, higher salaries, and better working conditions. Results were mixed, and strikes were frequent. It was a turbulent time for both labor and management.

Most of the advances in the regulation of child and female workers were the result of legislative action and not instigated by employers. In 1903, the general assembly passed an act that raised the minimum age for working in a factory or in the mines to fourteen years. The act also banned night work for children. Restrictions on child labor were further added in 1915 when, in addition to the minimum age, a child had to have finished seventh grade to be employed. The hours for child labor were changed to a maximum of nine and a half hours a day or a maximum of fifty-one hours a week, with no night work. And finally in 1935, a new act was passed, setting the minimum age for working at sixteen, with an eight-hour day and maximum of forty hours a week. No one under the age of twenty-one was allowed to work in a dangerous occupation.

Similar laws were passed regarding women in the workforce. For example, in 1913, the Women's Labor Law was passed, limiting the maximum hours of work for a female to fifty-four hours a week. The enforcement of the labor laws was another matter, and it wasn't until 1925 that the state created the Bureau of Women and Children to ensure that the current regulations were followed. Immigrants were not faring well in the work environment either, and in 1915 the state sanctioned a Department of Immigration and Employment to address the issue. It was a crucial measure as a large percentage of the industrial workforce at the time was from the immigrant population. In 1935, Governor Earle signed a new labor act that established the eight-hour work day, the forty-four hour work week, and other standards for child labor. This act, though frequently amended, is still in effect today.

The gradual decline of manufacturing capability in the state occurred as more and more of the plants moved to the Midwest and farther westward. One example is the auto industry, which settled in Michigan. Charles Duryea, maker of the first gas-powered automobile, had a factory in Reading, Pennsylvania, from 1900 until 1913, at which time he moved the factory to Saginaw, Michigan. Labor tended to be less expensive, and there was a large pool of labor to utilize.

INDUSTRIES

Agriculture

The agriculture industry in the state underwent several changes during this period. In 1900 there were 224,248 farms in the state; however, by 1945 that number had fallen to 173,267. One of the main reasons for the decrease in the number of farms was the consolidation of smaller farms into larger operations. By 1945, the average acreage of a farm in Pennsylvania had risen from seventy-eight acres in 1910 to eighty-three acres.

At the same time, the raising of livestock continued to fall—except poultry, which continued to be a major agricultural product in the state. Another exception to the general decrease of Pennsylvania livestock was the Hanover Shoe Farm, where horses have been bred for harness racing since 1926. In the area commonly classed as "principal crop products"—i.e., dairy, fruit, and vegetables, their production in the state ranked tenth in 1945. Apples and peaches were the top fruits produced by the state.

Computers

In the early 1940s, the Moore School of Electrical Engineering at the University of Pennsylvania received a contract to develop a computer. The team, led by Dean Harold Pender and Professor J. G. Brainerd, selected bright graduate students and began the work. In 1943, Presper Eckert and Dr. John Mauchy presented the plans for the first digital computer. In 1945, ENIAC (Electronic Numerical Integrator and Computer) was born. It was officially dedicated in early 1946 and represents the first electronic digital computer in the world.

Coal

The coal industry during this period can be characterized by three factors: frequent strikes, multiple mine disasters, and a weakened demand for anthracite coal in favor of gas or oil to heat the home. All three factors placed coal mining in a very weak position. Mine disasters were frequent and deadly. In an effort to create a more stringent control for mine safety, in 1903 Pennsylvania created the Department of Mines, but the effect was negligible. In 1907 there were the highest number of fatalities to date when 1,514 miners were killed. In one event alone, the Darr Mine disaster, 239 miners were killed.

However, as miners were gaining more benefits, the demand for anthracite coal continued to wane. In 1917, production topped 10 million tons, but by 1950, production had fallen to only 416 tons due to lack of demand. This was only six years after U.S. Steel opened the Roberta mine in Green County, at the time the largest coal mine in the world at a total of 22,000 acres or 34.9 square miles. Roberta operated until 1983 and was the world's first fully automated mine.

Media

Pennsylvania was very much in the forefront in written and spoken media. For years Philadelphia had been a major center for the publication of magazines and newspapers, and it continued to be so throughout the first half of the twentieth century. One early newsperson, Ida Tarbell, became very famous for her publication in 1902 of *The History of the Standard Oil Company*. It was a forerunner of today's investigative reporting. She continued her journalistic efforts and became a highly respected reporter at a time when female journalists were rare. Other media landmarks of importance include the following:

- Father Joseph Murgas, a Catholic priest in Wilkes Barre, is credited with inventing the forerunner of the radio. He obtained a patent for his invention in 1904. The equipment was very expensive to make, and the U.S. Navy in 1905 supported the radio made by Guglielmo Marconi, which could be made at a much lesser cost.

Nickelodeon Theater, Pittsburgh, 1905

◆ In 1905, the first motion picture theater in the world opened on Smithfield Street in Pittsburgh. The theater was called Nickelodeon and was opened by Harry Davis on June 19, 1905, to a first-day gate of 450 viewers. The next day, attendance more than doubled.

◆ On election night, November 2, 1920, the first commercial radio station in the world went on the air as KDKA in Pittsburgh. The broadcast was from a shack on top of one of the Westinghouse buildings—as it was sponsored by

Early photo of station KDKA in Pittsburgh

G. Westinghouse. The initial broadcast was continual from 6 p.m. of November 2nd until 1 p.m. of November 3rd. During that initial broadcast, listeners frequently heard the following announcement:

> "Will anyone hearing this broadcast please communicate with us, as we are anxious to know how far the broadcast is reaching and how it is being received."

Amateur operators were quick to respond, and KDKA broadcasts continue to this very day.

Merchandizing

Having sold his caramel company in 1900, Milton Hershey began to seek a place to establish his chocolate company. He finally settled on a small hamlet known as Derry Church in Dauphin County. Here he built his first factory and proceeded to create a company town unlike the classical company town. He installed libraries, shops, individual homes, and all the amenities normally associated with a town. He renamed Derry Church as Hershey, and his first factory came online in 1905. With his wealth, he opened the Milton S. Hershey School in 1909. The school opened with ten male students and has since grown to have over 1,100 girls and boys. The only criteria for entry are a financial need and a desire to learn. It is now a residential school for prekindergarten to twelfth grade and is the largest residential school of this type in the United States.

Meanwhile, in the western part of the state, Henry J. Heinz had built his empire as the maker of pickles, ketchup, and vinegar to be the largest manufacturer of condiments in the United States.

Roads

Pennsylvania early on had a relatively good system of roads. Most of the roads ran north and south and were located in the eastern part of the state. The invention of the gas-fueled automobile, which quickly became a "love affair" in the state, and the increase of both population and industry around the Pittsburgh area made an east-to-west road a priority. The popularity of the gas-fueled automobile increased in

First drive-in filling station in United States in Pittsburgh

the early part of the century, causing a demand for "filling stations." Recognizing this fact and seeing the inconvenience caused by having to fill your auto outside in all kinds of weather, the Gulf Oil Company opened the first drive-in filling station in the United States in 1913. The station was located on the corner of Baum Boulevard and St. Clair Street in Pittsburgh. It was an instant success.

As autos composed a more significant portion of the transportation system, it became apparent that better roads were necessary. In the late 1800s, William Vanderbilt had proposed a new highway between Philadelphia and Pittsburgh and even begun construction of the proposed road. The project ran out of money and went dormant until 1937. That year, under Governor Earle, the state legislature passed an act establishing the Pennsylvania Turnpike Commission. The proposed east-west turnpike would follow the route of the old South Pennsylvania Railroad and would not have more than a 3 percent grade on any stretch. The estimated cost of the project was between $50 and $70 million (actual construction costs were about $450,000 per mile). The federal government, through the Reconstruction Finance Corporation, provided a bond issue of $35 million, and an additional $29 million came from the Public Works Program.

The first stretch of new road opened to the public in September 1940. It consisted of 160 miles from Middlesex, a town near

Harrisburg, to Irwin, about fifteen miles from Pittsburgh. The turnpike was an immediate success. Shortly after World War II, the turnpike was extended from the eastern border to the western for a total of 337 miles. It was the first turnpike of its kind in the United States and an impetus for the Interstate Highway System, sponsored by the Eisenhower administration.

As the roads expanded, the state realized that an official Pennsylvania road map had become a necessity and issued one in 1925.

Steel

The steel industry in Pennsylvania underwent a major shift in the early part of the twentieth century. What had been an industry of both large and small mills became an industry of two giants. This came about in 1901 when Andrew Carnegie sold his steel company to what became known as U.S. Steel Corporation. The founding fathers of the new corporation were: Andrew Carnegie, J. P. Morgan, Charles Schwab, and Elbert H. Gary.

The corporation soon acquired many of the smaller mills, including America Steel & Wire Co., the National Tube Co., American Tin Plate Co., American Steel Hoops Co., and the American Sheet Steel Co. Virtually all of the mills were located within a one-hundred-mile radius of Pittsburgh.

The other major steel producer was the Bethlehem Steel Corporation, located in the eastern part of the state in Bethlehem. In 1904, Charles Schwab left U.S. Steel and joined Bethlehem Steel. Under his

Andrew Carnegie   J.P. Morgan   Charles Schwab   Elbert H. Gary

Founders of U.S. Steel Corporation

management, Bethlehem Steel soon branched out into shipbuilding and provided many vessels to the U.S. Navy in both world wars. The Bethlehem Steel plant notably provided steel for the construction of the Empire State Building, the Golden Gate Bridge, and both the Lincoln and Holland tunnels in New York.

The expansion and consolidations of the steel industry did not alleviate the early problems between the owners and the workers. In fact, it complicated the issue. Recognition of unions remained a very sensitive point, and it was not until 1942 that U.S. Steel recognized the United Steelworkers of America for negotiating purposes, and then only after a major strike by the workers that year caused a change in union/management relations.

The industry thrived, in part due to two world wars and the high demand for steel for use in weapons and transport. During World War II, the Pennsylvania steel industry produced 95 million tons of steel for wartime use. After World War II, the steel industry began to decline, as corporations were moving facilities farther west. This was only the beginning of the decline of the state's steel industry.

Textiles

Pennsylvania continued to manufacture carpets, hats, stockings, leather goods, and clothing throughout the early 1900s, where there was an abundance of female and child labor available. Those mills remained active.

THE INDIANS

The Carlisle Indian School received national attention during the early part of the twentieth century when the Apache chief Geronimo visited on his way to Washington for the inauguration of President Theodore Roosevelt. Geronimo had always wanted to come to Washington to speak with "the One in Washington," and Teddy Roosevelt allowed him off the reservation in Oklahoma for the visit, but always under guard. Geronimo was accompanied on his visit by chiefs

Geronimo parade in Carlisle in 1905 (Geronimo is in the center, without a headdress.)

of the Lakota, Blackfoot, Ute, and Comanche tribes. On March 2, 1905, Geronimo and his Indian contingent visited the Carlisle Indian School. Their visit was preceded by a parade through the streets of Carlisle with all the Indian Chiefs dressed in their Indian finery. The chiefs were Hollow Horn Bear (Sioux); Little Plume (Blackfoot); Buckskin Charlie (Ute); and Quanah Parker (Comanche).

That evening, Geronimo addressed the student body of the Indian School gathered in the school chapel. He said to the students:

> *My friends: I am going to talk to you a few minutes, listen well to what I say.*
>
> *You are all just the same as my children to me, just the same as if my children are going to school when I look at you all here. You are here to study, to learn the ways of white men, do it well. You have a father there and a mother also. Your father is here, do as he tells you. Obey him as you would your own father. Although he is not your father he is a father to you now.*
>
> *The Lord made my heart good, I feel good wherever I go, I feel very good now as I stand before you. Obey all orders, do as you are told*

*all the time and you won't get hungry. He who owns you holds you
in His hands like that and He carries you around like a baby. That
is all I have to say to you.*

The next morning, Geronimo, the other chiefs, and over three
hundred Indian cadets boarded a special train, went to Washington,
and were members of the inaugural parade.

Geronimo and the chiefs in their native dress made quite a contrast to the Indian cadets in their school uniforms. Geronimo did
get his chance to meet with President Roosevelt and plead his case
to allow his people to return to their native Arizona. President Roosevelt could not honor his request, as Geronimo was still a hated man
in Arizona.

The custom of having Indian representation at the presidential
inaugural was continued by president-elect Woodrow Wilson. He
invited thirty-two chiefs, representing eleven separate tribes to attend
his 1913 inaugural. En route to the ceremony, the chiefs visited Philadelphia, where they were entertained at the Wanamaker store. The
chief of the Blackfoot presented John Wanamaker with a necklace of
Buffalo teeth saying, "May you live as long as these teeth are old. I

1913 Indian delegation visiting John Wanamaker

now name you High Crow." Wanamaker was the first white man to be given honorary membership in the Blackfoot tribe.

At the time of the visit to the Indian School in Carlisle, there was a young Indian of the Sauk Fox tribe named James Francis "Jim" Thorpe there, who was destined to become one of the most famous athletes of his time. He specialized in track and football, and he was a champion in both sports. In 1911 and 1912, he received All-American honors for football, and in 1912 he was a member of the U.S. track team for the Olympics in Antwerp, Belgium. At those games he medaled in both the decathlon and the pentathlon. Unfortunately, the medals were stripped from him in 1913 when it became known that he had played semiprofessional football. The medals were not restored to the family until 1982. In 1920, Jim Thorpe was named the first president of the American Professional Football Association, which is now the National Football League (NFL).

Jim Thorpe

The Carlisle Indian School closed its doors in 1918, later to become the U.S. Army War College. Many of the original buildings have been preserved and are still in use today. Although the school closed, there was an Indian presence in Pennsylvania until the early 1950s.

The pre–Cold War period ends with a general feeling in the state that Pennsylvania was a major part of a larger organization known as the United States. Participation in two world wars had drawn the country together. Because of wartime production, Pennsylvania's economy was still going strong, and life was generally good for most Pennsylvanians. Residents of the state were very proud of the state's heritage and its prominent place in the history of the United States. Their state had been a key contributor in support of the national missions in both manufacturing and manpower. They were now ready to move on into a new peacetime environment.

CHAPTER NINE

FROM COAL TO ATOMS
(1950–2000)

NATIONAL

Post–World War II, Pennsylvania was marked by a shrinking population and persistent labor conflict. Both politically and economically, Pennsylvania was changing.

Politically, the postwar shift of population from Pennsylvania to the more western states became evident in the U.S. House of Representatives. With every census, Pennsylvania's delegation lost seats.

Census Year	PA Representatives in House	Ranking (Size)
1950	30	2nd
1960	27	3rd
1970	25	3rd
1980	23	4th
1990	21	5th
2000	19	5th

The population shift on the national scene was also evident in the world of manufacturing. In 1947, Pennsylvania ranked second in the United States in manufacturing, but by 1955, it had dropped to fifth.

On June 25, 1950, when the United States became enmeshed in the United Nations military involvement in Korea, the state of Pennsylvania responded to the call. The final count of Americans killed during the Korean War lists Pennsylvania with the most killed in action at 2,030, followed by California at 1,896. In 1961, Pennsylvania was called upon to supply service personnel for the Vietnam War, costing the state 3,139 residents. Army and National Guard troops from Pennsylvania also participated in both Desert Storm and later in Operation Enduring Freedom.

On the civilian front, on December 8, 1953, when President Eisenhower gave his Atoms for Peace speech at the United Nations, Pennsylvania took center stage on the national scene. In late 1954, ground was broken in Shippingport, Pennsylvania, for the United States' first nuclear power station. Eisenhower remotely activated the beginning of the construction with a ceremonial "neutron wand." The Shippingport Nuclear Power Station was a cooperative effort between the Duquesne Light Company, the Atomic Energy Commission (AEC), and Westinghouse. The design was based on the nuclear reactor used in the *Nautilus* submarine. Construction of the project lasted until late 1957 at a cost of $72.5 million. President Eisenhower participated in the site opening from the White House on May 26, 1958.

The site, located on the Ohio River approximately twenty-five miles from Pittsburgh, continued to operate until October 1, 1982. Pennsylvania had entered the nuclear age, and a controversy began in the state. People in the state were uneasy about having nuclear power in their backyards—the vision of Hiroshima was still too vivid a memory. Many needed to be convinced that the plants were safe and truly beneficial in the production of electrical power.

Shippingport Nuclear Power Station

President Eisenhower waves his "neutron wand" in Denver, Colorado, to remotely activate the construction of the Shippingport nuclear facility.

In 1958, the nuclear controversy came to the forefront again in the state as the result of an Atomic Energy Commission (AEC) initiative code named Project Plowshare. The project, announced in June of 1958, was designed for the specific use of nuclear energy as a tool in geographic engineering by employing underground nuclear blasts. Tests were conducted in New Mexico, and by 1968, considerations were given to commercial use of the technique. One of the proposed efforts was Project Ketch, located in Pennsylvania.

The plan proposed, in a cooperative effort between the AEC and Columbia Gas, the detonation of a twenty-four-kiloton nuclear bomb 3,300 feet underground to produce a storage area for natural gas. The site chosen was in the Renovo area of central Pennsylvania. When the plan was leaked to the press, Pennsylvanians reacted with anger, capturing national attention for their cause. In July of 1968 the project was cancelled.

As the Project Ketch furor subsided, in 1969, another nuclear event was just beginning—the construction of a two-reactor site at Three Mile Island (TMI). The construction on the first reactor began in 1968 (completed in 1974), and construction on the second began

Cartoon depicting reaction to Project Ketch

in 1969 (completed in 1978). Both reactors went online, and while TMI-1 functioned according to specifications, TMI-2 had a continual string of problems. The city of Harrisburg and its surrounding areas generally welcomed the TMI operation as the future for generation of electricity. For residents of the area, TMI represented the potential for technically qualified persons and indicated to all Americans that the city of Harrisburg welcomed new technology.

That all changed in the early morning hours of March 28, 1979, when at 4 a.m., TMI-2 experienced a "meltdown." While the meltdown was serious, it was not a worst-case accident. It was caused when the feed water pumps in the non-nuclear section failed, and the unit overheated. The event was immediately fodder for not only the national press in the United States but for news organizations around the world. Nothing like this had happened before. All experts and the Atomic Energy Commission declared that the meltdown was not considered dangerous to the local population.

Governor Thornburgh, working closely with the AEC and the U.S. Nuclear Regulatory Commission (NRC), assessed the damage to the reactor, and after three days, on March 31, 1979, declared the reactor damaged but not dangerous to the civilians in the area. He did, however, suggest the voluntary evacuation of pregnant women and young children. In all, over 200,000 people voluntarily evacuated the area near the reactor.

Three Mile Island reactor under guard

The meltdown of TMI-2 had far-reaching impact. The NRC established a tighter control for the inspection of nuclear plants, insisted on a more detailed evacuation plan for all areas near a nuclear reactor, and put in place many other safety initiatives. As for the TMI-2 plant, it was permanently shut down and defueled. It will continue to be monitored until its license expires and the plant is destroyed. The incident at Three Mile Island will forever be etched in the minds of the generation who lived through it, both in Pennsylvania and throughout the rest of the world.

It remains an event that the state of Pennsylvania would just as soon not have happened, but it also took the headlines from the coal industry in the state, much to the relief of the mine owners.

National attention again focused on Pennsylvania and Three Mile Island in 1996, when the U. S. Supreme Court refused to hear an appeal regarding TMI. The case focused on ten of two thousand physical injury cases filed against the owner of TMI—Metropolitan Edison Co., a subsidy of General Public Utilities (GPU). A class-action suit for the ten cases had been thrown out by the appeals court for insufficient evidence in 1979, along with the other 1,990 pending cases. After many years in the court system, the U.S. Supreme Court, in June of 1996, by not acting on the case, allowed an appeal court ruling counter to the original ruling to stand. The individuals could in fact sue the owners. After continual court action, all of the remaining

1,990 class-action suits were dismissed by the Supreme Court in December 2002. All of those cases were based on the "stress" factor which is difficult to prove. It should also be noted that in 1985, GPU paid out more than $14 million in out-of-court settlements.

After World War II, lack of adequate housing became a national issue, and Pennsylvania took the spotlight with a new concept of housing developed by William Levitt & Sons in Bucks County. The project, known as Levittown, was the first of a new concept—a totally planned community with space allocated for schools, churches, parks, and shopping centers. The community consisted of 17,300 homes with a peak population of 75,000 residents.

Originally Levitt refused to sell homes to people of color, thereby causing a national concern. Not until 1957 did the first African-American couple move into the community, only to be met with great animosity. Finally, after national pressure and several law-suits, the policy was changed. The concept of Levittown had a socio-logical impact beyond the racial issue—they were the first "planned" communities for middle-class families. Levitt set the model for the modern suburb.

In 2007, William Levitt & Sons filed for bankruptcy protec-tion. At that time, their emphasis was on the southeastern part of the United States, and that area was undergoing a major housing slump.

Levittown, Pennsylvania, 1955

INTERNAL

Realizing that the state constitution of 1874 needed amending, a Constitutional Convention was called in 1967 and 1968. The major amendments adopted as a result of the convention included the following:

- The general assembly would meet annually and be a continuing body.
- The governor and other elected state officials were eligible to succeed themselves for one additional term of office.
- A unified judicial system was established under the state supreme court.
- Denial of civil rights to any individual was prohibited.

By an Act of December 6, 1972, the state constitution, including the 1968 amendments, was declared to be known and cited as the Constitution of 1968.

The post–World War II period has not been kind to the state of Pennsylvania, due in large part to the collapse of the major industrial base of the state—coal and steel production. The effect of the collapse can be seen in the state population figures. From the time of William Penn until the industrial collapse, the state had experienced an average annual growth rate of 20 percent. That changed drastically—in 1950 the growth rate was down to 4 percent, and by the year 2000, the growth rate was virtually zero.

Industrial areas with a major shift in population are shown in the following table:

City	1974 Population	1990 Population
Easton	39,301	21,521
Johnstown	12,490	1,821
Monongahela Valley	69,749	18,775
Beaver Valley	29,874	9,321

Cities felt the population downturn as well as the outlying industrial areas.

Between 1940 and the year 2000:

City	% Population Loss
McKeesport	55%
Philadelphia	22%
Pittsburgh	50%
Scranton	46%
Wilkes Barre	56%

The economic impacts of the population changes for Pennsylvania were, and to some extent still are, extensive. Pennsylvania has, due to its current metamorphosis and lack of industry, become a state with a "gray population" (second only to Florida), as the young tend to leave for better employment opportunities. It also has the unfortunate distinction of having the lowest state percentage of children enrolled in public elementary and secondary schools—young families, too, are leaving.

The state, in reaction to the loss of its industrial base, is now endeavoring to develop a large part of its economy on "heritage tourism." Pennsylvania's natural landscape, history, and its diverse population provide a solid base for this endeavor.

INDUSTRIES

The post-1950 time period has not been kind to Pennsylvania's industrial base, and by 1958 the state had fallen from second to fifth among manufacturing states. The shift of industries to other locations where labor costs were less, the introduction of more modern techniques at new plants, and the lessening demand for coal all played a role in dismantling the manufacturing base of the state. The loss was dramatic. In 1969, Pennsylvania reported a manufacturing workforce of 1.58 million. By the early 1990s, that number had fallen to less than 1 million. Between 1979 and 1989, the state lost one-quarter of its manufacturing jobs. The "Rust Belt" became an appropriate term for the state's industrial area.

Agriculture

While the number of farms has decreased over the past fifty years, agricultural production for the state has increased. Presently there are over 59,000 working farms in Pennsylvania, with 4 million acres in agricultural production and another 4 million acres in woodlands and pastures. The state is also ranked seventh nationally for its production of non-citrus fruit. As more and more people move into the state, the demand for land to construct new homes has placed increased pressure on the agricultural community to reduce their farm sizes and sell portions of their farms to builders. Most of the development is occurring along the peripheral areas of the state, such as Adams County, where people can live in Pennsylvania and work elsewhere.

Coal

As the demand for coal continued to lessen, the coal mining industry in the state constricted. In just the twelve years from 1980 to 1992 the number of miners (anthracite and bitumen) shrank from 12,476 to 4,546—and the consumption totals dropped from 57,319 short tons (STs) to 45,414. The impact was deadly for many small towns in the coal mining regions of Pennsylvania. Natural events also affected the industry. In January of 1959, the Knox Mine was flooded by the Susquehanna River, causing the deaths of twelve miners. The costs of pumping the water out of the mine were prohibitive and the mine was closed, thereby closing the coal-mining industry in the Wyoming Valley.

Two issues continued to plague the coal-mining industry during this period. One was strip (or open pit) mining, and the other was the impact of long-wall mining. Throughout the period, both the national and state legislatures attempted to control open-pit mining, particularly in the area of restoration and water contamination. Open-pit mining is literally mining from the ground down into an open pit without tunnels. Long-wall mining, which had been used in Pennsylvania since the 1960s, produces about 50 percent of the coal mined and presented a different problem. Long-wall mining is favored by the mining companies as it is more economical and requires fewer miners. However, the technique of long-wall mining uses the coal veins as walls and allows the walls of the shaft to collapse after the coal is removed. This often causes what is known as subsistence to the land above—that is, sinking or shifting of the surface land, which in many cases can cause damage to personal property. In 1994, the state legislature passed Act 54, which allows coal companies to dig under surface structures built before 1966 as long as property owners are compensated for subsistence damage and water loss.

The use of the long-wall technique and the controversy over open-pit mining has led to an increase in underground production. In 1990, underground production was 40,330 short tons (STs), and in 1999 production had risen to 58,215 STs while the open-pit production numbers dropped from 29,984 STs in 1990 to 17,188 STs in 1999.

The coal industry, however, continues to survive, as coal is the primary source used by the utility companies for the generation of electricity.

Nuclear power

After the opening of the Shippingport nuclear reactor in 1957, the state began to study the wider use of nuclear energy as a source of electrical power. The interest grew into a reality beginning in the 1960s and is still very much a major source of electricity in Pennsylvania today. Thirty percent of the electricity input into the state's power grid is from nuclear sources.

The plants built after the Shippingport plant are all located along the Susquehanna River for its source of water. The Mississippi is the only river in the United States that has more nuclear plants along its shores than the Susquehanna. Pennsylvania ranks second among the various states in its use of nuclear energy as a source of generating electricity.

Current Operative Nuclear Plants in Pennsylvania

Reactor	Location	Operational Date
Peach Bottom	Lancaster	1967
Three Mile Island	Harrisburg	1968
Beaver Valley	McCandless	1976
Susquehanna	Berwick	1982
Limerick	Pottstown	1984

Pennsylvania Railroad logo

Railroads

The Pennsylvania Railroad, founded in 1846, had long been the largest railroad in the United States. Its logo was one of the most familiar in the world of transportation.

In the late 1950s the importance of the Pennsylvania Railroad waned as the Interstate Highway System was developed and Americans primarily used automobiles to travel. The rise of commercial air travel did not bode well for the railroad industry either. In 1968, the Pennsylvania Railroad, once the largest corporation in America, merged into the Penn Central Corporation, but that did not stop its inevitable demise. In 1970, the Penn Central Corporation declared bankruptcy, becoming, at that point, the largest business failure in United States history. The rail industry in Pennsylvania reduced its workforce by 25 percent between the years 1964 and 1972.

Steel

Up until the early 1950s, the steel industry was prosperous, and the word *steel* was synonymous with Pennsylvania. World War II and the Korean War had created high demand for steel products. However, the industry suffered from major strikes in both 1953 and 1959—the 1959 strike costing the steel industry over $6 billion in lost production and wages. The industry believed it could ride out the problems, but time proved them wrong. Labor issues, along with antiquated equipment and poor quality control, proved insurmountable.

After 1963, the industry went into a sharp decline, and its demand for protective tariffs against foreign steel was not heard by legislators in Washington. As the decline continued to deepen, the profitability of the industry substantially decreased. In 1970, U.S. Steel lost $56.1 million in one quarter alone. As the profits for the industry in general decreased, so did the workforce. In 1980, there were 90,000 steel workers in the Pittsburgh area; by 1984, that number had shrunk to 44,000. However, the steel industry did survive; for example, U.S. Steel now reports earnings of over 5 billion dollars a quarter and has a workforce of over 49,000 employees.

Homestead in Allegheny County is often cited as an example of the impact of the collapse of the steel industry in Pennsylvania. The town, the site of the famous Homestead Strike in 1892, was dependent on the steel industry. At its peak in 1946, Homestead had a population of just over 20,000, but by the year 2000, the population had decreased to a mere 3,569 as a direct result of the closing of the steel mill. There are many other similar examples of the negative impact the industry's decline in the state has had on the small towns surrounding steel mills.

In 1996, national legislation was passed to create a Heritage Trail to commemorate the steel industry in Pennsylvania's history. Historical sites are located in Allegheny, Armstrong, Beaver, Fayette,

Logo of the rivers of steel heritage area

Greene, Washington, and Westmoreland Counties—all previous centers of the steel industry.

Textiles

The textile industry suffered the same geographic shift as that of coal and steel. The silk mill industry that had flourished in the state since 1873 met its demise in 1989, when the Catoir Silk Mill closed in the Lehigh Valley. At its peak in 1920, Pennsylvania had three hundred mills employing one-third of all the silk workers in the United States.

THE INDIANS

After the closing of the Carlisle Indian School in the early 1900s, there was only one remaining vestige of the American Indian in the state of Pennsylvania—the Seneca reservation known as Kinzua in the Warren County area near Lake Erie. This land had been recognized in the Canandaigua Treaty of 1794 as the property of the Seneca Nation. The land was protected by Article III of the treaty, which states:

> Now, the United States acknowledge all the land within the aforementioned boundaries, to be the property of the Seneca Nation; and the United States will never claim the same, nor disturb that Seneca nation, but it shall remain theirs, until they choose to sell the same to the people of the United States, who have the right to purchase.

The treaty signed by Timothy Pickering for the United States and Chief Cornplanter, along with fifty-nine other chiefs of the Six Nations, remained basically intact until the late 1950s. At that time, the federal and state governments, being concerned about the consistent flooding problems in the area, requested the Corps of Engineers' assistance to solve the problem. The result was a recommendation to build a dam in the Kinzua area for flood control. This meant terminating the treaty regarding the Seneca Nation land—as the land would be taken by eminent domain.

The Friends Society (Quakers) filed a lawsuit in federal court to prevent the taking of the land, but it was thrown out by the federal courts, and the Supreme Court refused to hear the case. The case eventually arrived on President Kennedy's desk, and, while sympathizing with the Seneca's cause, he refused to act on their behalf.

In total, 550 Seneca Indians were forced off their reservation. They moved to the Salamanca reservation in the state of New York. Along with the move of the families, the grave of their famous Chief Cornplanter was also moved to safe ground. The Indians were compensated for the land by a $15-million payment from the federal government.

The resulting dam is the largest dam east of the Mississippi. It took five years—between 1960 and 1965—to build the dam at a cost of $109 million. The dam flooded over ten thousand acres of Seneca land and rendered another twenty thousand acres essentially useless because of the new flood plains established. The site is now a popular recreational site. However, many of the people who visit the site fail to realize that the forced removal of the Seneca Indians from their reservation at Kinzua represents the final vestige of the Native American's presence in the state of Pennsylvania, treaties notwithstanding.

From 1950 to 2000, the decrease in workers from the coal-mining and steel-manufacturing areas was dramatic. At the same time, the state in general was experiencing what many of the other thirteen original colonies were experiencing—that of a shift of industry to the western states.

CHAPTER TEN

PENNSYLVANIA TODAY

Today, Pennsylvania is in a transitional stage, changing from an industrial giant to a state with a more varied and complex economy and workforce. As the shift of the industrial base continues, the county population gains and losses also reflect the changing environment of the state.

Between 2000 and 2003, four counties saw growth rates of over 5 percent:

Pike County	12.7% growth rate
Monroe County	11.5% growth rate
Adams County	5.7% growth rate
Chester County	5.5% growth rate

It is interesting to note that all of the counties with major population growth are located in the eastern section of the state and are adjacent to major population centers, the neighboring states of New York, Maryland, and New Jersey. In contrast, of the six counties that lost more than 2 percent of their population, only one is located in the eastern part of the state—Philadelphia. The other five counties are all located in the central or western part of the state, predominately in areas known for the production of steel or coal.

Cameron County	−3.3% growth rate
Philadelphia County	−2.5% growth rate
Warren County	−2.4% growth rate
Elk County	−2.3% growth rate
Cambria County	−2.1% growth rate
Sullivan County	−2.0% growth rate

In total, between 2000 and 2003, thirty-three counties experienced a positive growth percentage ranging from 0 to 12.7 percent, while thirty-four of the counties experienced a negative growth percentage ranging from 2.1 percent to 3.3 percent.

While the population and industrial centers may be shifting, the state of Pennsylvania remains committed to the basic principals developed by its founder William Penn. Religious tolerance, the value of education, development of the arts, and a firm commitment to the form of state and local government (i.e., boroughs, townships, counties) all still prevail.

As the country becomes more mobile, Pennsylvania has realized the value of both its natural and historic resources, leading to an increased effort to develop the state's tourist industry. Areas of interest span the entire state, from the historic sites in the east to the Rivers of Steel in the western part of the state.

At the national level, while Pennsylvania has seen a decrease in its delegation to the U.S. House of Representatives, it still continues to be a loud voice in the nation. Its nickname, the Keystone State, is as appropriate today as it was when initially given. Its population is known to consist of solid, hardworking citizens—Americans to the core.

Seal of the State of Pennsylvania

The state seal is used to authenticate certain state documents. The seal was adopted by the general assembly in 1791. The obverse side of the seal contains a shield crested by an American eagle. The shield contains a ship, a plough, and three sheaves of wheat. To the right of the shield is an olive branch, and on the left is a stalk of Indian corn. On the reverse side is a woman representing liberty. In her left hand she holds a wand topped by a liberty cap, the French symbol of liberty. In her right hand she holds a drawn sword. Under her feet is a lion representing tyranny. The inscription around the edge reads, "BOTH CAN'T SURVIVE."

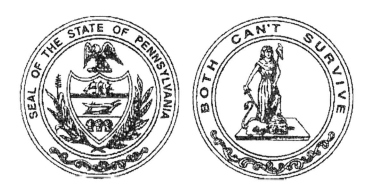

EPILOGUE

The state of Pennsylvania has a long history. It is a history that has affected not only the citizens of Pennsylvania but the citizens of the United States, as well as those in other far-flung areas of the world. While most Pennsylvanians are quick to remember the role played by the city of Philadelphia in the Revolutionary War, it should be remembered that in the late 1700s Philadelphia was the second largest English-speaking city in the world—second only to London. It was a city of culture and of constant innovations in the field of science and manufacturing and, most important, the birthplace of our American form of government.

Over time, the focus of the state shifted from predominately the eastern part of the state to the west. Pittsburgh became a major industrial center—one that was important on the national as well as state level.

It is a fair statement to make that Pennsylvania has transitioned from the "keystone" colony and one of the original thirteen states to a mature status among all the fifty states. Pennsylvania is not the manufacturing giant it once was, nor the governmental center it was in the time of the early United States, but it remains a state that is held in high regard by all the other states of the union. Pennsylvania will always be known as the Keystone State and will always respond to the call of supporting our United States.

A short and concise history of Pennsylvania cannot possibly deal with all of the events that occurred since the first white man came in 1638, but it can serve a vital purpose. Readers reading this history may find specific events that arouse their interest for more details—that makes this work worthwhile and useful not only to citizens of

Pennsylvania but also to readers throughout the United States. In the history of Pennsylvania, the younger states will find that this state experienced many of their same problems at an earlier time, and the solutions to the problems may help shed light on a more modern time.

The history of Pennsylvania continues . . .

GOVERNORS OF THE STATE OF PENNSYLVANIA

Presidents of Supreme Executive Council to 1790

1777–1778 Thomas Wharton Jr.
1778–1778 George Bryan
1778–1781 Joseph Reed
1781–1782 William Moore
1782–1785 John Dickinson
1785–1788 Benjamin Franklin
1788–1790 Thomas Mifflin
(None of the presidents of the council had a stated political party affiliation.)

Governors since 1790

Name	Dates Served	Party
Thomas Mifflin	Dec. 1790–Dec. 1799	None
Thomas McKean	Dec. 1799–Dec. 1808	Dem/Rep*
Simon Snyder	Dec. 1808–Dec. 1817	Dem/Rep
William Findlay	Dec. 1817–Dec. 1820	Dem/Rep
Joseph Hiester	Dec. 1820–Dec. 1823	Dem/Rep
John Andrew Shulze	Dec. 1823–Dec. 1829	Dem/Rep
George Wolf	Dec. 1829–Dec. 1835	Dem/Rep
Joseph Ritner	Dec. 1835–Jan. 1839	Anti-Mason
David Rittenhouse Porter	Jan. 1839–Jan. 1845**	Dem/Rep
Francis Rawn Shunk	Jan. 1845–July 1848	Democrat
William Freame Johnston	July 1848–Jan. 1852	Whig
William Bigler	Jan. 1852–Jan. 1855	Democrat
James Pollock	Jan. 1855–Jan. 1858	Whig
William Fisher Packer	Jan. 1858–Jan. 1861	Democrat
Andrew Gregg Curtin	Jan. 1861–Jan. 1867	Republican
John White Geary	Jan. 1867–Jan. 1873	Republican

Name	Dates Served	Party
John Frederick Hartranft	Jan. 1873–Jan. 1879***	Republican
Henry Martin Hoyt	Jan. 1879–Jan. 1883	Republican
Robert Emory Pattison	Jan. 1883–Jan. 1887	Democrat
James Addams Beaver	Jan. 1887–Jan. 1891	Republican
Robert Emory Pattison	Jan. 1891–Jan. 1895	Democrat
Daniel Hartman Hastings	Jan. 1895–Jan. 1899	Republican
William Alexis Stone	Jan. 1899–Jan. 1903	Republican
Samuel Whitaker Pennypacker	Jan. 1903–Jan. 1907	Republican
Edwin Sydney Stuart	Jan. 1907–Jan. 1911	Republican
John Kinley Tener	Jan. 1911–Jan. 1915	Republican
Martin Grove Brumbaugh	Jan. 1915–Jan. 1919	Republican
William Cameron Sproul	Jan. 1919–Jan. 1923	Republican
Gifford Pinchot	Jan. 1923–Jan. 1927	Republican
John Stuchell Fisher	Jan. 1927–Jan. 1931	Republican
Gifford Pinchot	Jan. 1931–Jan. 1935	Republican
George Howard Earle	Jan. 1935–Jan. 1939	Democrat
Arthur Horace James	Jan. 1939–Jan. 1943	Republican
Edward Martin	Jan. 1943–Jan. 1947	Republican
John Cromwell Bell Jr.	Jan. 1947–Jan. 1947	Republican
James Henderson Duff	Jan. 1947–Jan. 1951	Republican
John Sydney Fine	Jan. 1951–Jan. 1955	Republican
George Michael Leader	Jan. 1955–Jan. 1959	Democrat
David Leo Lawrence	Jan. 1959–Jan. 1963	Democrat
William Warren Scranton	Jan. 1963–Jan. 1967	Republican
Raymond Philip Shafer	Jan. 1967–Jan. 1971	Republican
Milton Jerrold Shapp	Jan. 1971–Jan. 1979****	Democrat
Richard Lewis Thornburgh	Jan. 1979–Jan. 1987	Republican
Robert Patrick Casey	Jan. 1987–Jan. 1995	Democrat
Mark S. Singel	June 1993–Dec. 1993*****	Democrat
Thomas Joseph Ridge	Jan. 1995–Oct 2001	Republican
Mark Stephen Schweiker	Oct. 2001–Jan. 2003	Republican
Edward G. Rendell	Jan. 2003–Present	Democrat

*Dem/Rep abbreviation for Democrat-Republican
**First governor elected under Pennsylvania constitution of 1838
***First governor elected under Pennsylvania constitution of 1874
****First governor elected under Pennsylvania constitution of 1968
*****Acting governor

Bibliography

Articles

Baumgartner, Nancy W., and Brasington, Marie. "Planting Churches in Frontier Pennsylvania." *Pennsylvania* 27.7, No. 5.

Bordewich, Ferguys M. "Digging into a Historic Rivalry." *Smithsonian*. Feb. 2004.

Brown, Leslie. "Nine Months in York Town." *Greater York*, 1996.

Ciervo, Art. "Paoili Memorial Marks Revolutionary War Massacre Site." *Pennsylvania,* Vol. 83 Sept./Oct. 2003.

Fein, Judith. "America's First Hospital." Pennsylvania, Jan./Feb 2004.

Jenssen, Thomas C. "The Forgotten Revolution, Women and Telegraphy in Pennsylvania." 2004.

Miller, S. James. "Up & Over–Crossing the Allegheny Mountains in the 19th Century." *Pennsylvania* 27.

Rich, John W. "Inferno on the BB&K Railroad, 1884 Tragedy Strikes Outside Bedford." *Pennsylvania* 26.

Periodicals

Pennsylvania Archaeologist, Bulletin of the Society for Pennsylvania Archaeology, Vol. 65, No. 1, March 1995.

Pittsburgh Geological Society, *The Flooding in Western Pennsylvania*.

Books

Ann Belharz. *The Allegheny Senecas and the Kinzua Dam—Forced Relocation through Two Generations*. University of Nebraska Press, Lincoln, NE, 1998.

Dunaway, Wayland F. *A History of Pennsylvania*. Prentice-Hall, Upper Saddle River, NY, 1948

Fortenbaugh, Robert. *The Nine Capitals of the United States*. Maple Press, San Jose, CA, 1973.

Graybill, Guy. *Keystone: A History of Pennsylvania*. Ironhorse Publishing, Midland, TX, 2003.

Miller, Randall M., and Willima Pencak, eds. *Pennsylvania, A History of the Commonwealth*. Pennsylvania State University Press, University Park, PA, 2002.

Schehr, Elizabeth, ed. *The Pennsylvania Manual (Volume 117)*. State of Pennsylvania, Harrisburg, PA, 2005.

Schmedlen, Jeanne H., ed. *The Capitol, A Palace of Art, Architecture and History*. The Pennsylvania House of Representatives, Harrisburg, PA, 2004.

Internet

Afrolumens project, *Fugitive Slave Incidents in Central Pennsylvania* (2005) www.dickinson.edu/department/history

American Industries, *Baldwin Locomotive Works* (2005) www.scripophily.net/ballocwor

American Revolution, *Timeline Revolutionary War* (2004) www.ushistory.org/March/timeline

ASME, *Shippingport Nuclear Power Station (1950)* (2006) www.asme.org/communities/history/landmarks/shippingport_nucler_power.ctm

The Avalon Project, *Declaration and Resolves of the Continental Congress* (2004) www.yale.edu/lawweb/Avalon/resolves

The Avalon Project, *Charter of Privileges Granted by William Penn, Esq. to the Inhabitants of Pennsylvania and Territories, October 28, 1701* (2004) www.yale.edu/lawweb/avalon/state/pa07

BBC, *The Burning of the Columbia-Wrightsville Bridge* (2005) www.bbc.co.uk/dna/h2g2 /A1112347

Brigniagra, *Niagara History—The Battle of Lake Erie* (2004) www.brigniagara.org/battle

Cyclopaedia of Political Science, *The Buckshot War* (2004) www.econlib.org.LIBRARY/YPDBooks/Labor/lCy1962

Doc Heritage, *The Horseshoe Curve* (2005) www.docheritage.state.pa.us

DuBois, *The Negro in Philadelphia 1920–1896* (2004) www2.pfeiffer.edu/~iridener/DSS/DuBois/pnchiv

Encyclopedia of North American Indians, *Cornplanter* (2003) www.indigenouspeople.net/cornplanter

Gettysburg National Military Park, *Lincoln and Gettysburg* (2005) www.pueblo.gsa.gov/cic_text/misc/gettysburg/g.

Grenoble, *Frame of Government Pennsylvania* (2004) www.yale.edu/lawweb/avalon/states

History of Wyoming Country, *French and Indian War–Early Settlement* (2003) www.polsci.wvu.edu/wv/wyoming/wyohistory

Historic Valley Forge, *Timeline Leading to Valley Forge* (2004) www.ushistory.org/valleyforge/history/timeline

Internal Revenue Service, Frequently Asked Questions (Indians) (2005) www.irs.gov/govt/tribes/article/0,,id=108394,00

Irish Society, *The Philadelphia Nativists Riots* (2004) www.irish-society.org/hedgemaser%20archives/phi

IUP Special Collections & Archives, *Kinzua Dam* (2002) www.lib.iup.edu/spec_coll/exhibits/saylor/kinzuadam

Lehigh Coal and Navigation Company, *A Freight Car Was America's First Roller Coaster* (2004) www.pennhomes.com/historyofchambersburg

Modern American Poetry, *About the Carlisle Indian Industrial School, by Barbara Landis* (2003) www.english.uiuc.edu/maps/poets/a_f/erdrich/boarding/carlisle.

National Atlas, *Congressional Apportionment* (2006)
    www.nationalatlas.org/articles/boundries
National Park Service, *The First Battlefield Park (1890–1899)* (2005)
    www.nps.gov
Pagefire, *Causes and Effects of the Whiskey Rebellion* (2004)
    www.assortment.com/whiskeyrebellion_rzjj
Penn National, *History of Chambersburg* (2005)
    www.pennhomes.com/historyofchambersburg
Pennsylvania Coal Statistics 1990–1999 (2006)
    www.alpha.org/trends_natural_resources.pdf
Pennsylvania Department of Environmental Protection, *First
    Anthracite Coal Burned in Grate, by Justice Fell, February 11, 1898*
    (2004)
    www.dep.state.pa.us/dep/deputate/enved/go_with_inspector/
    coalmine/Anthracite_Co.
Pennsylvania Historical and Museum Commission, *Swedes in Penn-
    sylvania* (2004)
    www.phmc.state.pa.us/ppet/swedes/page1.asp?secid=31
Pennsylvania Negro, *Legislation, etc. of Pennsylvania Regarding the
    Negro* (2004) www2.pfeiffer.edu~iridener/DSS/DuBois/appb
Pennsylvania State Archives, *Records of the Proprietary Government*
    (2005) www.phmc.state.pa.us/bah/dam/rg/rg21
Pennsylvania State Legislature, *The Era of Industrial Ascendancy 1961–
    1945* (2005) www.phmc.state.pa.us/bah/palhistory/industry
Pennsylvania State Legislature, *Independence to the Civil War, (*2004)
    www.phmc.state.pa.us/bah/pahistory/civil.asp?secld
The Pickering Treaty with the Six Nations, *The Canandaigua Treaty*
    (2002) www.canandaigua-treaty.org/The_Canandaigua _
    Treaty_of_1794
ePodunk Inc., Pennsylvania Population Changes, 2000–2003 (2006)
    www.epodunk.com/top10/county/pPop/coPop33
Post Gazette, Health, Science & Environment, *How Longwall
    Mining Works* (2003)
    www.pennslyvania.sierraclub.org/PAChapter/Issues/lon

Reader's Companion to American History, *Iron and Steel Industry* (2005)
www.college.hmco.com/history/readerscomp/rcah/html/ah_
046100_ironandsteel

Salisbury Area Industry, *The Coal Industry* (2002)
www.salisburypa.com/industry

Salisbury Area Industry, *Logging Industry* (2002)
www.salisburypa.com/industry

Snyder County, *Jurisdictional Chronology* (2003)
www.courts.state.pa.us/OpPosting/Supreme/out/J54-2003mo.p

State of Pennsylvania, Dept. of Mines, *A Brief History of Coal Mining Reclamation and Regulation in Pennsylvania* (2004)
www.dep.state.pa.us/dep/subject/advcoun/MINREC/MRAB_2

Tuscaroras, *About the Iroquois Constitution* (2003)
www.constitution.org/iroquois

U. S. Dept of Labor, Mine Safety and Health Administration, *District 1: Coal Mine Safety and Health, History of Anthracite Coal Mining* (2004) www.msha.gov/District/Dist_01/History/history

U. S. Nuclear Regulatory Commission, *Fact Sheet on the Accident at Three Mile Island* (2006)
www.nrc.gov/reading_rm/doc-collection/fact-sheet/3mile-isle

U.S. Senate Reference, *Chronological Table of the Capitals* (2003)
www.senate.gov/reference/reference_item/Nine_Capitals_of_
the_United_States

Vanderbilt University, *Supreme Court Allows Three Mile Island Suit to Proceed* (2006) www.vanderbilt.edu/radsafe/9603/msg00022

Wikipedia, the Free Encyclopedia, *Molly_Maguires* (2005)
www.Wikipedia.org/wiki/molly_maguires

Wikipedia, the Free Encyclopedia, *The Stourbridge Lion* (2003)
www.wikipedia.org/wiki/stourbridge_Lion

Wikipedia, the Free Encyclopedia, *Jim Thorpe* (2006)
www.wikipedia.org/wiki/jim_thorpe

World War II, *World War II, Korea, and Vietnam Casualties (by State)* (2006) www.army.mil/cmh-pg/documents/misc/stcas

PAMPHLETS

(These can be obtained by going to: Pmc.state.pa.us/bah/dpsi/ browse.asp?/catid=8.)

Pennsylvania Department of Environmental Protection, *Anthracite Coal Mining* (2004).

Pennsylvania Historical and Museum Commission, Historical Pennsylvania Leaflet 1, *The Pennsylvania Canals* (1992).

Pennsylvania Historical and Museum Commission, Historic Pennsylvania Leaflet 2, *Anthony Wayne, Man of Action* (1976).

Pennsylvania Historical and Museum Commission, Historic Pennsylvania Leaflet 5, *The Conestoga Wagon* (1997).

Pennsylvania Historical and Museum Commission, Historic Pennsylvania Leaflet 6, *The Fight for Free Schools in Pennsylvania* (1976).

Pennsylvania Historical and Museum Commission, Historic Pennsylvania Leaflet 7, *Thaddeus Stevens: Champion of Freedom* (1977).

Pennsylvania Historical and Museum Commission, Historic Pennsylvania Leaflet 8, *Pennsylvania's State House and Capitols* (1969).

Pennsylvania Historic and Museum Commission, Historic Pennsylvania Leaflet 9, *Harrisburg, Pennsylvania's Capital City* (1969).

Pennsylvania Historic and Museum Commission, Pennsylvania Historic Leaflet 10, *Pennsylvania and the Federal Constitution* (1969).

Pennsylvania Historical and Museum Commission, Historic Pennsylvania Leaflet 12, *The Amish in American Culture* (1972).

Pennsylvania Historical and Museum Commission, Historic Pennsylvania Leaflet 13, *Young Washington in Pennsylvania* (1997).

Pennsylvania Historical and Museum Commission, Historic Pennsylvania Leaflet 15, *Henry Bouguet and Pennsylvania* (1991).

Pennsylvania Historical and Museum Commission, Historic Pennsylvania Leaflet 15, *The Lattimer Massacre* (1997).

Pennsylvania Historical and Museum Commission, Historic Pennsylvania Leaflet 16, *The Battle of Lake Erie* (1996).

Pennsylvania Historical and Museum Commission, Historic Pennsylvania Leaflet 17, *Armstrong's Victory at Kittannying* (1995).

Pennsylvania Historical and Museum Commission, Historic Pennsylvania Leaflet 18, *Benjamin Franklin* (1992).

Pennsylvania Historical and Museum Commission, Historical Pennsylvania Leaflet 19, *The Allegheny Portage Railroad* (1993).

Pennsylvania Historic and Museum Commission, Historic Pennsylvania Leaflet 20, *Abraham Lincoln and Pennsylvania* (1977).

Pennsylvania Historical and Museum Commission, Historic Pennsylvania Leaflet 22, *Edwin I. Drake and the Birth of the Modern Petroleum Industry* (2002).

Pennsylvania Historical and Museum Commission, Historic Pennsylvania Leaflet 22, *Ida Tarbell* (1997).

Pennsylvania Historic and Museum Commission, Historic Pennsylvania Leaflet 23, *Pennsylvania in the Civil War* (1998).

Pennsylvania Historical and Museum Commission, Historic Pennsylvania Leaflet 24, *The Walking Purchase* (1972).

Pennsylvania Historical and Museum Commission, Historic Pennsylvania Leaflet 25, *Albert Gallatin, Master of Finance* (1962).

Pennsylvania Historical and Museum Commission, Historic Pennsylvania Leaflet 26, *William Penn in Pennsylvania* (1995).

Pennsylvania Historical and Museum Commission, Historic Pennsylvania Leaflet 27, *Conrad Weiser* (1998).

Pennsylvania Historical and Museum Commission, Historic Pennsylvania Leaflet 28, *James Buchanan* (2000).

Pennsylvania Historical and Museum Commission, Historic Pennsylvania Leaflet 29, *The Underground Railroad* (1995).

Pennsylvania Historical and Museum Commission, Historic Pennsylvania Leaflet 30, *Centennial Exhibition of 1876* (1969).

Pennsylvania Historic and Museum Commission, Historic Pennsylvania Leaflet 31, *Pennsylvania Archaeology: An Introduction* (1994).

Pennsylvania Historical and Museum Commission, Historic Pennsylvania Leaflet 32, *Chief Cornplanter* (1972).

Pennsylvania Historical and Museum Commission, Historical Pennsylvania Leaflet 33, *Pennsylvania's Roads before the Automobile* (1972).

Pennsylvania Historical and Museum Commission, Historical Pennsylvania Leaflet 34, *Pennsylvania's Roads: The Twentieth Century* (1972).

Pennsylvania Historical and Museum Commission, Historic Pennsylvania Leaflet 35, *The Liberty Bell* (1993).

Pennsylvania Historical and Museum Commission, Historic Pennsylvania Leaflet 36, *Simon Cameron* (1974).

Pennsylvania Historical and Museum Commission, Historic Pennsylvania Leaflet 37, *The Battle of Brandywine* (1992).

Pennsylvania Historical and Museum Commission, Historic Pennsylvania Leaflet 38, *The Battle of Germantown* (1974).

Pennsylvania Historical and Museum Commission, Historic Pennsylvania Leaflet 39, *Gifford Pinchot* (1976).

Pennsylvania Historical and Museum Commission, Historic Pennsylvania Leaflet 40, *The Battle of Wyoming and Hartley's Expedition* (1976).

Pennsylvania Historical and Museum Commission, Historic Pennsylvania Leaflet 41, *Sullivan and Brodhead Expedition* (1976).

Pennsylvania Historical and Museum Commission, Historic Pennsylvania Leaflet 43, *Child Labor in Pennsylvania* (2005).

Pennsylvania Historical and Museum Commission, Historic Pennsylvania Leaflet 44, *Agriculture in Pennsylvania* (2001).

Pennsylvania Historical and Museum Commission, Historic Pennsylvania Leaflet 45, *Radion in Pennsylvania* (2002).

Pennsylvania Historical and Museum Commission, Historic Pennsylvania Leaflet 46, *The Civil Rights Movement in Pennsylvania* (2004).

Pennsylvania Historical and Museum Commission, Historical Pennsylvania Leaflet 47, *Railroading in Pennsylvania* (2003).

Tritt, Richard L., *Geronimo and Carlisle* (undated).

Index

Tammany (Delaware chief), 40
Tarbell, Ida, 152
textile industry, 84–85, 121–122,
    157, 175
Thorpe, James Francis "Jim," 160
Three Mile Island, 165–167
treaties, 21–22, 41, 42
Treaty of Easton, 42
Treaty of Lancaster, 41
Trenton Decree, 33

Unami. *See* Lenapes
universities
    Pennsylvania State University, 75
    University of Pennsylvania, 38
    University of Pittsburgh, 75
U.S. Steel Corporation, 156, 174

Valley Forge, 57, 58, 59
Virginia, 32

Wanamaker, John, 114–115,
    159–160
War of 1812, 70, 74
Weiser, Conrad, 22–23
Welsh immigrants, 34
Westmoreland County, 24
Whig Party, 30, 76–77, 101
Whiskey Rebellion, 54, 55
Wilmot, David, 71, 96
Wilson, James, 48, 52
Women's Medical College
    (Philadelphia), 123
World War I, 135–136
World War II, 140–141
Wyoming Valley, 32, 36, 59–60,
    61, 171

York County, 35, 103–104
York, Pennsylvania, 46, 47, 103
Yuengling Brewery, 135, 136, 137

Breinigsville, PA USA
14 September 2009
223962BV00004B/11/P

9 780781 811972